Teachings of the

Tree of Life

Other books by Father Peter Bowes, many available on
audio and recorded by the author, including:

❧

The Way, the Truth and the Life:
The Autobiography of a Christian Master

Pearls of a Fisherman

Spiritual Astrology I & II

The Word Within

Sayings of a Christian Master Teacher

Love is Simple

Pebbles on the Beach

The Joy of Stretching

Sermons from the Valley Volumes 1-3

Audiobook of The Gospel as Revealed to Me by Maria
Valtorta, Volumes 1-10

Father Peter Bowes

Teachings of the
Tree of Life

Sophia Publishing

Woodstock, IL

Teachings of the Tree of Life

Second Edition

ISBN: 978-1-387-50209-7

Sophia Publishing

509 E. Kimball Ave.

Woodstock, IL 60098

Cover Art: Ljiljana Mlinarevic

CONTENTS

Think of the solar system as the space and expanse of the mind of God and that within this boundary exist the twelve planets and that this entire space is filled with the ARCHITECT of the solar system. The SUN is the visible manifestation of the ARCHITECT of this solar system. The sun is the focal point of the manifestation of God, the Mediator of his intelligence and energy. The supreme beauty and good of human beings is the imitation of God that manifests with the Buddhist as the imitation of the Buddha and with the Christian as the imitation of Christ. The Christ within is the focal mediator within us.

The first commandment is: "I am the Lord your God, and you shall have no other gods before Me." There is a reason for this. God is the one Mind and Selfless Creator and all that is in the substance of being. The Creator is Self-less because alone God senses not, that is not in the dense world. Only through the actions and senses of human beings can God attain the joys and sorrows of dense matter. You might ask, "Why would God want to experience these sensations after experiencing the bliss in the realm of higher vibration, which is so much greater?" Why are we concerned about life if we are only a channel for God's experience?

In the School of Delphi, there was an immortal bit of wisdom given, "MAN, KNOW THYSELF." Another statement that comes from antiquity is, "AS ABOVE, SO BELOW." If you will take these two statements and sit quietly in thoughtful meditation, or just sit and think about them, you will learn much.

The purpose of life is to be a spiritual being in a spiritual world of reality with the objective of experiencing joy, and giving continuous joy by and through God, the Creator. The Bible says in Revelation 4:11, **"You have created all things, and for your pleasure they are and were created."**

4

The world we live in unfortunately appears so distrustfully reactive. The only hell we will ever know is our own. Therefore, our joy should start in this dense world by helping to relieve the apparent disorder of those around us.

Jesus says in Luke 11:52, **"Woe unto you, Conventionalist, for you took away the key to the sacred science; you did not go in and those who were about to go in you prevented."** This is the real science of life you are about to study.

Meditate on these daily:
Monday: In God's Mind do we (God and I) create all things in my life.
Tuesday: In God, I rest.
Wednesday: With God, all things are possible.
Thursday: In God, I rest.
Friday: This is the way I accept my supply and good this day from God.
Saturday: I love, through action, my brothers and sisters.

CREATOR II

We call these studies a science because they relate to the use of the tools God gave us and how to use the power of God in its various manifestations. Science comes from the Latin root "scio," which means "to know." Many people react to the above statement that this attitude toward God is cold and feelingless. But that is not what they are really saying. They are saying that we are making this God a real, dynamic force and power, and that if I do not get my prayers answered, then I must look to myself to see what is wrong with my thinking, and I can't blame God for it. In other words, there are no alibis, and there is no room for excuses.

Where there is Law and Order, there is science and an overall pattern, and things in the act of being created. On the earth plane, there is an ebb and flow of all things. "As above, so below." It is true in the microcosm of the human heart as well as in the macrocosm of God, the Whole, the One Mind. Our heartbeat's diastole and systole is in harmony with the blood's ebb and flow – a rhythmic pattern – as in the inspiration and expiration of the lungs or the psychic body's throbbing with the electromagnetic energy of the spirit. The ocean tides go in and out, day succeeds night, seasons arrive and pass, ages of time incline and decline, constituting eons of time.

So vast is this latter conception that we are careless about retaining it in consciousness and tend to dismiss it from consideration. We have the same attitude about abstractions, such as the vagueness of a poetic statement about the life of the gods, having little relevance to our everyday life. Involution and evolution forever succeed each other and may be known in the wide, horizontal view as the heartbeat, the ebb and flow of the manifestations of God. Time itself does not exist in God's world, but time in the plane of earth's limited substance is but the tick-tock in God's time.

Remember, God geometrizes, for geometry is but the numerics of form. When God created the world, his first thoughts were expressed in numbers.

Socrates said, "Philosophy is the way to true happiness, the offices thereof are two: to contemplate God and to abstract the soul from the corporeal sense." Socrates lived 500 years before the Master Jesus was here. Somehow we feel that this business of getting acquainted with God is a new thing; and in a most abstract sense, it is, for the conditions electrically, mentally and physically from all sides are different. It is a case of whether you really want the peace taught by the Master Jesus, or must your ego be fed?

The first step to understanding the great creative power GOD is to experience it. Energy is power, it is that which the Spirit motivates; it is the life force after it has taken on the characteristics of the Christ. You are using energy every moment of your life – it is light – it is God in action. We could not live without energy. It is manifest on every plane and in all the multiwaves. It is all there is. Be consciously aware of this mighty force and consciously try to work with it. The greatest of all mysteries is God's consciousness in us.

When we speak about life, we are dealing with the power of God flowing through the Son. In every religion there are people who are serious about their relationship to God, even if it is called by another name. We need to be very respectful of people's religious beliefs, since they all point to one Source. For some God may manifest as sunlight, the song of birds, the cooing of a newborn baby in its mother's arms, but it is one and the same God.

We must learn to feel God's presence moving through us. Know that it is here, not in some far-off, distant heaven. The ancients considered this of first importance because if you do not feel the presence of the Father, how can you communicate with Him? The ancient Greek philosopher Plotinus said, "There exists nothing in this universe, or this solar system, but God." We know the ego will not like this, but whether it does or not will not change the fact. Mass mind thinking tries to ignore the light of wisdom Plotinus gave to the world, the same as with the words of Jesus. If you speak about God, you are always thought to be speaking about some external and impersonal God. This is absurd – because there is no place in nature for such a God. Everything is created by the internal activity of God's consciousness.

No one can see their own face without the use of a mirror of some kind. Likewise, God, when starting a cycle of activity, cannot see God's Self without some substance to reflect in. There is no other substance except that which belongs to God's consciousness to serve as a mirror. Thus, God steps out of Himself, out of his own center, for Self-examination, and looks within. A conscious being is created by God perceiving the images existing within its own substance. So, the activity near the center, its radiant field, created in the Universal Mind a place to reflect God's own image. This is the demonstration of "As Above, So Below." This is also the way we pray, by direction of our thoughts to our own center, the center of God's consciousness in our hearts.

Ezekiel 18:14 **"Behold, all souls are mine, the Soul of the Father as well as the Soul of the Son is mine; the Soul that sins shall die."**

The material world is the world of appearances. We are interested in appearances only because they are reflections of the patterns in the unseen world. Our attention must be on what intended behind the appearances. Is our perception perfect? The object perceived may be different from the mind perceiving it. We would then have an image instead of the true picture in the mind of God. But our minds are able to perceive the ideal truth exactly as it is. We are not able to study this as something external to us. It is within us. Consciousness is the sole basis of certainty. The mind is its own witness. Our mind sees in itself that which is above itself as its source and again, that which is below itself once more. It is a fact that God does exist because we can only know what God knows in God's Mind, as our mind is only an individualized part of God's Mind. God is a material fact in the realm of God's level of consciousness.

Meditation: Close your eyes and contemplate these truths:
Monday: I cease to think of God as external. It is within me.
Tuesday: It is I who is in the universe, and not on it or merely of it.
Wednesday: The consciousness of God is life, but it is more: it is love, and it is power unlimited.
Thursday: The greatest attribute is love. Love is creative and protective.
Friday: Love is inspiring and illuminating; therefore it gives life and light.
Saturday: I will consider myself as the light of the life, in the love of God with God.

MEDIATOR

A mediator is a go-between, one who interposes between two parties in order to harmonize or reconcile them. The great Christ is the Mediator of this solar system. The Christ diffuses to all of creation the light, life and love of God.

On earth, Jesus Christ and Mother Mary are the Co-Mediators between us and the great Christ. Jesus says, **"Only through Me will you see the face of the Father."** Through Jesus and Mary's consciousness and mantle, we can reach the great reality of ourselves and God.

The term "go-between" points out the realness of the Lord Jesus and his function for us. We have lost all consciousness of life and of the great Creator of the life. We struggle to have two cars, two houses, a good-paying job, an attractive partner and all other worldly goods. Our whole existence is wrapped up with ourselves. We can no longer reach out of ourselves to see the world as it truly is. For even as we walk down the street, we see the buildings and those passing by through our own thoughts and with all of our biases and narrow-mindedness. We do not even see a fourth of the material world. We just see through our own distorted filter.

The use of a go-between allows us to see past the misconceptions of the world and penetrate into the greatness of the Creator without opinion and prejudice. The Mediator links the two together, being on earth, but giving out the truth, the light and reality of the one mind. Jesus said in the New Testament, **"For, truly, I will be with you until the end of the Age."** He is ever-present and always at hand, unifying human beings with the Creator. He is a channel of the great light and wisdom of God for the earth.

In prayer, when we reach our mind, heart and soul upward to the Father, we travel through these great Masters, for Jesus

11

and Mary have given themselves as a channel for the Word. We could no longer stand the light or the truth of God, so there were placed for us Mediators who brought things down to our level so we could access them and understand them. By our act of harmonizing ourselves with these Mediators, we become in harmony with the one for whom they mediate, God.

Jesus said, **"I am the Way, the Truth, and the Life."** He took on the greatness of God while here on earth so that we could see it. After the Ascension, his spiritual body diffused around the earth and became the mystical body of Christ. Everyone who receives the light of Christ becomes a living, moving, active cell within this body. The ruler of the whole body is the Godhead. To attune to the Mediators, we must follow implicitly all of God's directions that bring forth out of the depths of our being the great love for our Creator.

If we observe the condition of the world today, we can easily see that the creative power has been misused. There was so much fear and confusion that without some help, we would all perish and cut ourselves off from God. A mediator was necessary to channel the reality of things, to show us how things are supposed to be and what is possible. The dictionary defines "mediator" as "something intermediate; a middle state or degree; an intervening thing through which a force acts or an effect is produced; any means, agency, or instrumentality."

I Timothy 2:3-5 **"This is good and acceptable in the sight of God our Savior, who desires us to be saved and to come to the knowledge of the truth. For there is one God and there is one mediator between God and human beings, the man, Christ Jesus."**

The world needs an awakening. The love and power of God that should be manifesting itself through us is absent. Sin is transgression of the Law. It is also ignorance of the Law. The Law is spiritual. It is the Law of Karma, or the Law of Cause and Effect. The Law is the functional way the mind of God works. Whatever we put out, we get back. As we give, so do we receive. When a person, who is also spirit, violates the Law, the spiritual state of mind is disturbed. Our denial of truth and acceptance of appearances only has caused separation from God. A false state of consciousness swoops down over the creation and lulls it to sleep, known in very severe states as death.

The divine Son of God must become the Herald, the Messenger and the Mediator. The Herald shall declare, **"Arise and Shine! For the Glory of the Lord is risen upon the earth."** The Mediator seeks and saves that which is lost. "Christos" translated means "Anointed Savior."

Once we are fully aware of our creatorship, we begin to mediate between light and darkness, between the apparent and the real. This is not to say that the dense world around us is not to be mastered and worked with but that the Law of God is changeless and eternal. The cause of what is apparent is the Law working through the mind and our pronounced word given to us by the Creator.

Paul says in I Timothy 1:8, **"Now we know that the Law is good, if anyone uses it lawfully."** Understand this! The Law is not laid down for the just but for criminals and the disobedient. The children of earth today are disobedient. That is why all have sinned and fallen short of the glory of God.

The Mediator, also called the Son of Righteousness with healing in his wings, brings the Law into manifestation. The infallible Law changes the atmosphere from a negative cycle to a positive cycle, transforming heaven out of hell. Since Paul says, **"Be transformed by the renewing of your mind."**

Jesus says, **"I and my Father are one." "I go to prepare a place for you and I will come to get you, that where I am, you may be also."**

Though the power operates through our physical body, which is symbolized as the Son of God, it is still another form of mind. For mind is the primal will for good, the operator of the Law. Salvation is the cleansing and perfecting of you, individually, through Christ. We are the congregation of the earth gathered in the outer court of the temple of life. The divine human being is the Master. Those who have become enlightened and perfected are the High Priests after the Order of Melchizedek.

Read Hebrews 7 and keep it in mind while reading the following so that your understanding may be increased.

1. Know that a real Order of Melchizedek does exist.
2. Our bodies are the Temple.
3. Our will and personality, the Lamb of God for sinners slain.
4. Our hearts are the Altar.
5. The Law operating through us is the High Priest.

By enlightenment of mind, strengthening of will, singleness of purpose, we can save and unite the world, the entire Cosmos, through Jesus Christ and Mary, the wayshowers, the first among many. Christ must return and is returning. The return of Christ will be complete – the return of Law and Order, Peace, Joy, Justice, Love and Compassion. The divine Self will reconcile us to the infinite Law of Creation.

The key that makes us one with the Mediators is the manifestation of the Christ mind in us. That is why Paul said, **"Let this mind be in you, which was also in Christ Jesus, who walked not after the flesh, but after the Spirit."** In conclusion, to be finite-minded, or lawlessly-minded, is death. But to be spiritually minded is life. In Adam, we die; but through Christ, we are made alive.

14

CREATION I

How was our solar system created?

According to John 1:1, **"In the beginning was the Word, and the Word was with God, and the Word was God. God was in the beginning with God; all things were made through God, and without God was not anything made that was made."**

We are trying to understand God through the Bible, the philosophies and now through science. All of our strivings seem to culminate in what we examine in the material world. Theories that leave out God and the creative power of God eventually become abandoned because they are incompatible with observed results. Our personal understanding of the origins of this solar system will not bring us any closer to the original truth than our general understanding of nature.

Until we know what we are, until we know the Self, we cannot conceive from whence we came, or for that matter how the world formed. Until we know who we are as souls, we must admit that we are speculating. First, let it be understood that there are no destructive acts in the mind of God. We know the solar system is continually building itself up to complete the original Word of God, evolving order out of Chaos. Non-existence will never come. There is only the transformation of energy from one form to another – some in denser forms, some more refined, some seeable, some unseeable. We know that everything is a fundamental part of the same being – God.

Time is a point in the relativity, both in relation to cyclic motion and the state of density. When this takes place in one state of frequency, we have a dimension of time related to that particular time. Events are vibrations with a position in space. Time is seen as a transient flowing framework of matter, events and living substance. Think of time as nothing more than such a series of events with an interval of recurrence shorter than the minimum interval of sensual perception. Simply put, there is no such thing as space in this solar system, and that what science is calling "space" lies in concentric layers around the sun in this solar system. Light radiates from its source and is globular. The measurement of the speed of light is another test made under minor conditions. In other words, 186,324 miles per second is very much relative to other straight-line paths, measured in our atmosphere.

Time is the result of periodic alternations or vibrations. A solar day is a primary period – the period of light and darkness that the Bible speaks about. A solar sun cycle is a second degree of time as the sun swings north and south of the equator. The earth's cycle around the sun is another. All other measurements are subdivisions of these factors. Time does not exist except as a relative standard within a particular dimension.

The first cause means the first Word spoken by the Father. The process of creation means the evolution of harmonious secondary vibrations from the primal one. It is the continually sounding Word of God, producing all forms and harmonies. This universal vibration can be measured. The fundamental universal vibration is the one known as the "Constant," which is a vibration of 3.29×10^{15}-power cycles per second. It corresponds to a calculated wavelength of 911.27×10^{8}-power centimeters. This is the fundamental frequency, or internal frequency of both the positive and negative electrons that are the primary units of matter.

One of the laws of vibrating bodies is that it sets up harmonic vibrations at intervals of one octave, or at a point of successive doublings plus half of the fundamental frequency. In a musical sense, these harmonic notes are the closest thing to the fundamental vibration. A cell is a persisting condition of electrical tension in free vibration within the body of a larger cell. The larger, organized combination of molecules, or cells, and human beings have a higher fundamental frequency. The universe or world cell has the highest of all. It is possible to calculate the fundamental frequency of the world cell and of human beings.

Vibration has three characteristics: frequency, position and amplitude. The study of vibration resolves into the study of numbers. In music, the division into halves, fourths and squares form an energizing and disagreeable beat frequency. The division into thirds form harmonious musical sounds, as in primary colors or planetary aspects. Squares and oppositions in astrology are inharmonious, while trines and sextiles are harmonious. Again these are the fours and the threes. Twelve is the product of the harmonious three and the discordant four and so contains both elements. Six is a combination of three and two. Eight is all twos. Nine is all threes.

A common tendency is to count by twelves, like a dozen, twelve inches, twelve signs of the Zodiac; 360-degree circles are equal to twelve 30-degree sections. The solar day is a standard unit of time, so it is a natural frequency.

From the one vibration of God's Word come all the musical tones, colors and all of Creation. Even the heartbeat, the breath, the life periods, the moon periods and the movements of the planetary bodies work in this way.

Creation has three orderly stages: 1. Formation; 2. Growth; 3. Perfection.

Formation: Genesis 1:26 **"Then God said, 'Let us make man in our image, after our likeness and let them have dominion over the fish of the sea and over the cattle and**

over all the earth and over every creeping thing upon the earth.'"

"Let us make the human in our image." This shows that people were made with all the ability of God and the nature of God. We were put in the position of a god over the animal kingdom and over all the earth. We can now look around and see the earth for which we are all responsible.

Genesis 2:7 **"Then the Lord God formed the human of dust from the ground, and breathed into his nostrils the breath of life and the human became a living being."** The term "formed" shows that something else was used, not just the physical substance.

Growth: Colossians 2:19 **"And not holding fast to the head from whom the whole body nourished and knit together through its joints and ligaments grows with a growth that is from God."** Our body is what our mind determines; the body grows by the power of God. We are the physical aspect of the Creator. We are the ones through whom the spoken word becomes flesh. We are God's vehicle of expression. These lessons will teach you to live and move and have your being in the creative Word.

This supports the saying that the Law works whether we are aware of it or not, for we are using it every day if we are living and breathing. The secret of this lesson is found in Genesis 1:9, **"And God saw it was Good."** We must be able to see nothing but good in manifestation, around us and especially in our world, our personal atmosphere.

We wish to emphasize at this time that we do speak and not merely affirm the "Word." 1. Speaking the Word of power is as different as night is from day. 2. Speaking the Word of power makes you the Creator, not an empty boat in a storm-tossed sea.

Colossians 1:15 **"He (Jesus) is the image of the invisible God."** For in God all things were created in heaven and on earth, visible and invisible, whether thrones, dominions, principalities or authorities - all things were created through God and for God. Though Paul was speaking of Jesus, he also revealed the secret that we are also capable of this. For Jesus said, **"Of these things I do so will you do also and greater things than these."**

We partake of the same divine nature. As creators we can recognize nothing else but that divine nature of the God of creation. There is simply nothing else to recognize. Paul declares in verse 19, **"For in Him all the fullness of God was pleased to dwell."** Since it refers to Jesus, it naturally refers to the sons and daughters of God, as Jesus is our elder brother. We are joint heirs with Christ. Therefore, we also are sons and daughters of God.

This is a Law, an immutable fact, indivisible, eternal in the heavens in all this solar system. Using this knowledge and the power contained, we open a door that a person can shut. In case of necessity, we can shut a door that no one can open. Compare John 1:1, **"In the beginning was the Word and the Word was God..."** with Genesis 1:1, where it says, **"In the beginning, God created..."**

Jesus showed us the power of the spoken Word through many of the healings He did and by producing the food that fed the 5,000 and many other miracles. These were done by speaking the Word of power. John 11 shows where Jesus spoke the Word to Lazarus, saying **"Lazarus, come out,"** and you know that Lazarus did arise and was healed, right now.

CREATION II

In God there exists a directive intelligence, a sustaining life and a creative will. God embodies these three powers to support all life and assist human beings on this planet. In Egypt and Greece, they are called "gods," in the East, "devas," and in the West, "Angelic Hosts."

Spiritual teachings and modern science agree that the universe consists of energy, that all matter is energy. This is the domain of the spiritual hierarchy. For these beings are fundamentally directors of universal forces and power agents of the Logos (Word), God's engineers of the magnificent process of creation. Creative energy is being perpetually poured out. It passes through the bodies and auras of the hierarchy on the way to material manifestation. In this process, it is transformed, or "stepped down" from its primordial potency. Thus, the creative hierarchy is a transformer of power.

The higher worlds, which are inhabited by the hierarchy, consist of matter of increasing tenuousness, ranging from the density of the finest ether up to the rarest and most spiritual condition. Highest among the spiritual hierarchy, or the aspects of God fully manifested, are the seven solar Archangels – the Seven Mighty Spirits – which include the well-known Michael, Gabriel, and Raphael. Michael has dominion over protection and removing darkness and negation. Gabriel has dominion over communications and connecting God with the creation. Raphael has dominion over healing and the movement of the Spirit of God. This is just a small manifestation of their power and energies in the hierarchy of God.

The ministry of angels has been an accepted teaching of all the religions, and a living reality to a great many people. During such ministrations, certain orders of angels at once appear as the natural agents of those forces being used. Their function is to conserve and direct the forces generated by ceremonial action, prayer and adoration, and to serve as channels for the power and the blessing that descend in response. This ministration is far more effectively carried out when recognized by both ministrants and those assembled.

In church services and group meditations, these attending angels minister and help with the progress of the participants. While ceremonies intelligently performed are one of the most effective means of cooperation between angels and human beings, these are not required. For the human mind is, itself, a powerful broadcasting and receiving station. Given the power of a strong will with training in concentration, and illumined by intuitive knowledge of the unity of life, the person becomes an extremely potent instrument.

Whenever a human thought is strongly directed toward one particular order of angels, the mental signal being dispatched is received by members of that order. If we have attained a definite universality of consciousness, and our motive is entirely selfless, the angels will unfailingly respond. We may then direct our thought power into our chosen field of work, assured of angelic cooperation. Their active cooperation may involve such ministrations to others as spiritual healing, inspiration, protection, or helping someone to overcome a weakness of character. Collaboration may also be sought in order to gain the inspiration required to perform certain altruistic work.

Angels can be powerful allies who have the ability to open up channels of inspiration between higher consciousness and the brain, and to convey telepathically a train of illuminating ideas to minds that are receptive. Continued practice of invoking the help of the angels has been found to produce a change in the human aura, the link thus formed being visible as an area of brilliant light vibrating at the higher frequencies that characterize the auras of angels. When this "devic seal," as it is called, has been quickened by ceremonial action, or by thought and will alone, it transmits a signal on the wavelength of that particular order of angels whose aid is being invoked. This call is then picked up by the corresponding angels in terms of vibratory frequency and they are at once ready to help.

Clairvoyance is useful in this process but not necessary. Regular practice, based on intuitive recognition of the truth of these ideas, will quickly provide convincing evidence of the reality and effectiveness of cooperation between ourselves and angels. This cooperation is constantly occurring in the realm of our higher Self, however unaware of this fact the lower self may be.

The Archangels, which in Christian terminology are called "Thrones," find it their special mission to inspire nations through their higher Selves. Under these conditions of angelic inspiration, the statesperson becomes possessed of powers not previously suspected. As long as they serve their nation, this power will grow. But, should selfish interests intervene, the angelic and other inspiration would be withdrawn and power soon decline.

For one week, pray to a particular Archangel and feel the presence of that great being.

PRAYER I

Prayer is heartfelt devotion to God. When we want to have a conversation with God, we will clear our minds and focus our whole attention on God within. Then we will speak and say what is in our heart and what we feel we want. Prayer is an intimate conversation with the most trusted, respected friend that we can ever hope to have. God will respond if we are open, humble and loving because God wants to be close to us. As we get closer to God, God draws closer to us, and we form a lasting, solid relationship of love.

The perfect prayer should contain praise, glory and worship to the Creator.

In Matthew 6, Jesus says, **"...For yours is the kingdom, and the power and the glory."** The perfect prayer contains thanksgiving to God for our many blessings. It also contains our requests for the things we require, desire, wish and want. Jesus said, **"Whatsoever you ask in my name shall be given to you."** The Law of Prayer works scientifically in that we get results each and every time. This demonstrates the consistency of the giving of the Creator, that all we ask for is given us.

The method for asking for what you want is this: Before you pray, know what you are going to pray for. Know in detail what it is you want. Draw a mental picture of what you need, for there can be no confusion in your mind as to what you want. Then, establish contact with the Father. When this contact is established, you can feel it, for God is closer than your hands and feet. Getting in contact with God is like contacting your friends. When the phone rings, the person on the other end of the line clicks on and you know that contact has been made without them saying a word. Thought is the transmission between you and God.

When you have established contact, ask for what you want or need. You ask in the name of our Lord Jesus Christ. Then, as Jesus said, **"Whatsoever you ask in my name shall be given to you."** What you have asked for is then yours. It has already been given to you, so you go on about your business and forget about it, or as we say, you let go and let God. Then thank God for what you are being given, as it is God's power that brought this into your life.

The Law of Prayer is shown in the symbol of the triangle: Shown graphically it looks like this:

FATHER

HOLY SPIRIT   MEDIATORS (SUN/SON)

When you contacted God, you were at the uppermost part of this triangle, the Father. When you asked for what you wanted, you moved your consciousness from the God point of the triangle to the Mediator(Sun) point of the triangle. When you received what you asked for, this is shown in the motion from the Mediators through the Holy Spirit point of the triangle. The Master Jesus manifested the second point of this triangle that St. John called the Logos, or the Word. The Son is the eternal Word of the Father. At this point of the Law, we use the Word as Jesus said, **"The Father gave to Me the Word, so I give it to you."**

The triangle shows the action from God to the Mediators, then to the Holy Spirit. So, in using the Law, we must start by contacting God. Jesus talked about the Pharisees in the New Testament, how they would stand on the street corners and make long, beautiful prayers so that those around them would hear them. They forgot to contact God, for if they had, their prayers would have been fulfilled.

The science behind Jesus' statement **"Whatsoever you ask in my name shall be given to you"** is "nature abhors a vacuum." Your asking creates a vacuum that shall be fulfilled. A vacuum is a space or something that is missing. The Word creates the physical vacuum that is physically fulfilled.

The Law of Prayer is also extremely simple. If we would use pure logic, the reasoning of a child, we would have known God and would have all our prayers answered.

Prayer is our most powerful tool. It makes it possible for us to govern our lives and control our personal universe, accepting into our life what we desire and rejecting all negative things for our health. For we are not a ship on a stormy sea being tossed to and fro at the slightest whim. We are a creator who designs our own destiny. For without the knowing and use of the Law of Prayer, it is impossible for us to be the creators we are.

The definition of prayer: the scientific lifting up of our hearts and minds to God, the Creator. We pray in two forms: vocally and mentally. Vocal prayer is speaking the words out loud. It is necessary to voice our prayer because it sets up a certain vibration that can be measured scientifically. Vocal prayer centers our focus and causes a certain rhythm that aids our concentration. Luke 11:2 **"When you pray, SAY..."** Matthew 7:7 **"ASK, and it will be given to you; seek, and you will find..."** Matthew 6:9 **"Pray then like this: Our Father, who art in heaven..."** This will show the importance of voiced prayer.

Mental prayer is silent and uses the mind of God to create. Prayers must be creative and positive. In John 17, Jesus says

27

that God gave Him power over all flesh, to give eternal life to all whom God had given Him, and that He (Jesus) has given this to us, who are part of his Mystical Body. This is one of the most spiritually exalting chapters in the Bible to show our divinity. In verse 20, Jesus goes on to say that He prayed not only for the elect but also for those that became chosen through the acceptance of God, knowing that God was in them as they were in God, thus becoming one with God. Here, again, this is a voiced prayer of Jesus.

The use of prayer brings into our lives the manifestation of the presence of God. We understand that prayer is talking to God, and meditation is the process of receiving an answer. Contemplation is the process of revelation of our prayer. Meditation is the formula through which it works. Contemplation is the laboratory where the science of prayer and meditation are analyzed and proven scientifically correct. That which violates basic metaphysical laws, such as the Law of Cause and Effect, also violates spiritual law.

To understand more about giving praise, glory and thanksgiving, you may want to study a few Bible passages: Psalms 50:14, 69:34, 9:2, 28:2, 95:2-6, 102:18, 104:35, 106:1, 138:4, and 145:10; Matthew 2:2, 4:10, 6:13, 15:36, 21:16, and 26:27; Revelation 11:17 and 5:14; Romans 12:1; Acts 3:8 and 13:2; John 12:43; Luke 2:13; Exodus 24:16, 35:18, 40:34, 16:7, and 16:10.

PRAYER II

It is foolish to pray to God to cure a disease while we continue to violate some natural law that has caused it. We cannot ask the Creator to suspend temporarily the laws, through some outstanding miracle. We must have faith in the perfection, magnificence, and immutability of God's laws and of God's power. The mystic knows that God will never revoke or even slightly modify any one of the fundamental laws existing in the universe. Therefore, we never ask God to set one of them aside. But the mystic may pray, will pray, and otherwise bring about a different form of manifestation of the Law consistent with the purpose and motive in back of the action of the Law.

A person discovered that whenever lightning struck the lightning rod on the roof of his home, the water in his well was purified because the rod had a slight connection with the water pipes. He produced only a change in the manifestation of the fundamental Law by putting the end of the lightning rod down into the well itself so that the whole well full of water would be clarified by the action of the lightning. The fundamental Law was that the lightning would go to the ground, and there spend itself harmlessly. But he directed the Law so that it would not only spend itself harmlessly but constructively in purifying the water. Did he change a fundamental Law? Or, did he direct the Law into a different manifestation by looking at the secondary principles involved and directing them?

When we discovered that water dropping over a cliff had power to destroy things beneath its weight, we invented the water wheel and hydroelectric power so that the Law in the action of dropping water would manifest differently, constructively, instead of destructively. No Law was changed, but other laws were properly applied to the fundamental one.

This is the work that the mystic does. It is the work we must do in the attainment of mastership over the finite part of our existence.

Prayer is the lifting up of heart to the Creator in words. Words produce a rate of vibration, rhythm, measurable as it leaves the body. Voice is a sound. The whole system vibrates creation, rhythm. The pulse of the body varies. We set it in motion, and it does the work.

MEDITATION: O soul of me, do reveal in retrospection as I am in the eyes   of the Cosmic. Let me sit alone and keep silent. Amen.

Paul told Timothy in the New Testament, **"To study, to show himself approved a workman, not needing to be ashamed, but rightly dividing the word of truth."** Paul also said, **"pray without ceasing."** It is a good example of conclusive, supplicative prayer. It is the prayer that was prayed by Jesus in John 17.

The Law is the most important facet of prayer. For the Law can become the nature of one's own Spirit and is the spiritual essence of this Law. King David said, **"I delight in your Law, day and night."** This is prayer without ceasing. In Matthew 7:21, **"Not everyone who says to Me, 'Lord, Lord,' shall enter the kingdom of heaven, but those that do the will of my Father which is in heaven."**

Will power is necessary in using the Law of prayer. After we have praised, worshipped and glorified God, after we have thanked God and asked for what we want, we use our power to bring into manifestation the pattern, thing or relationship we want to manifest. Then the will of God will manifest because the Father wants to give you the kingdom.

Setting the Law of prayer in action consists of expecting, affirming its presence and doing. In this, you move out on the physical plane as if you could already put the answer in your pocket. You have made yourself accessible to receiving it. After you have done this, you must go about acting as if you really knew your prayer was already answered affirmatively.

Matthew 7:7 says, **"Ask, and it shall be given you; seek, and you shall find; knock, and it shall be opened to you."** Analyze this statement. Look at the changes it can bring in your life. Put it to the test! See the effect of the action of the Law. When the Law of asking is put into effect, the result is that it will be given. The Law says: "Knock." When you do this, the result is that it will be opened. The Law says: "Seek." And when you have sought, you will find. Because there is no such thing as a negative prayer. There is not and cannot be a negative answer to prayer. Remember! You will reap what you have sown. The effect of a fervent, righteous prayer will be: everyone who asks receives; those who seek find; and to those who knock, it will be opened.

We are sure that after studying these lessons, you will find something useful in the words of the apostle James, **"The effectual, fervent prayer of a righteous person avails much."** He also said, **"Be doers of the Word, and not hearers only, deceiving yourselves. For if anyone is a hearer of the Word and not a doer, they are like a person who observes a natural face in a mirror, for they observe themselves and go away, and at once forget what they are like. But those who look into the perfect Law, the Law of Liberty, and perseveres, being no hearer that forgets but a doer that acts, they shall be blessed in their living."**

A prayer to meditate upon:

"Blessed is the light. Shower on me your ray. For as I travel in the darkness of this world of mine, I beseech you to illuminate my path. I petition You, O Christ, to lead me into your midst and that I may be filled with light. For to my light, I ask that my sisters and brothers may add their light. With the help of the ancient Masters and Ascended Ones, I ask to be filled with light so that I may find my way to God.

I, mortal body, need this divine strength that I may face in reality the sins of the past. That, when I am ready to look upon the God of my being, and see the glory of all creation, I will then have the strength to turn my back on the world and accept the Eternal Divinity."

If we raise enough feeling, confirmation and realization within ourselves, the prayer will get through the inner spirit of our being. The power is flowing through us and pictured or imagined.

Pray just once. Don't peek back over your shoulder at it. But you can reaffirm a prayer if needed. Meditation is the vehicle or formula through which prayer works. If we want something bad enough, and voice it, the Law will open the door.

I now realize:

1. Oh mortal body, that you are the densest form and vehicle of God-Self.
2. Oh mortal body, you are transitory.
3. You can deceive me no longer, for you are only what the real Self makes of you.
4. My soul, I am only what you are. All else is a passing fancy like the image in the mirror.
5. Therefore, I command my outer being to humble its ego, and cast aside the veil and permit me to express from within. For God is within, and without. We are inseparable.

Check to see if you followed the steps to prayer:

1. Did I really want what I was asking for?
2. Did I make contact and give over to God's presence and power?
3. Was my mental image or picture clear?
4. Did I let go? Did I accept the fulfillment of my prayer in my life?
5. Did I stop thinking about it and stop doubting whether it will happen?
6. Did I affirm it knowing that it was already done?
7. Did I examine closely to see whether it has already manifested?
8. Am I stepping out on my prayer and making myself available to it?

MEDITATION I

An excellent time for planting suggestions in the subconscious is late at night, just before going to sleep. At night we have the opposite condition from the morning: fatigue, congestion of thoughts, and a myriad of fleeting ideas trying to occupy our mental attention. Here we must willfully clear the brain and thoughts to make ready for the wonderful mental state of sleep. During sleep the brain is inactive, operating only the autonomic functions. If the sleep is deep and we are really relaxed, the subconscious mind has a greater opportunity to carry on its activities because it is not hampered by the incoming impressions from the conscious mind.

If, just before going to sleep, we willfully cast out all thoughts and concentrate our whole attention on some idea and fall asleep with this one idea occupying our consciousness, it will pass from our brain, or conscious mind, to the subconscious, firmly implanting this idea.

But we need a formula to do it, and our thought must be in the form of a suggestion. It must be so visualized and worded that it is not merely a vague, abstract idea. It must be a specific command, worded something like this: "Tomorrow I will do this or that;" "Tomorrow I will accomplish this or that." If the idea we wish to hold in our mind before we sleep is in regard to something we wish to do the next day, we need to visualize ourselves doing the act.

This way we are really commanding our subconscious mind to accept this statement as a decree. It will be received by the subconscious mind in that form during our sleep and it will become a law, a paramount law, an absolute law within the mind and will be so established there by morning that it will be the first thing our conscious mind contacts upon awakening. We will feel the effects of it all day as an inner command and inner reminder of what we are to do. The thoughts coming from within during the day will be an inspiration and will give us confidence to proceed to do what we wish to do.

We have two periods, early morning and late at night, when we are most susceptible to the influence of suggestion. At other times, when we are in a meditative or relaxed state, if we can get away long enough to look out a window into space, or at some trees or flowers, or into some dark corner of our home, and go into meditation, we will feel rejuvenated. When we are lost in this spell of meditation or reflection, this thought in the form of a suggestion or command will slip from our conscious mind into the subconscious mind and take form. The more completely we forget our environment and forget where we are for two or three minutes, and have nothing but the one thought inhabiting our whole awareness, the more completely and commandingly will the idea and suggestion pass on to the subconscious mind.

Do this during the coming week and learn the first principles of Self-mastery.

Just as Prayer is talking to God, Meditation is listening to God.

Mediation begins the real spiritual work. Mediation is the art of keeping the conscious mind on one thing so the Divine Mind can come through. The conscious mind must be held in stillness so the Divine Mind can pour in its wisdom and information. If our conscious mind cannot concentrate on one thing only, it is like being tuned to two radio stations at the same time. We will receive only garbled static.

All terms we use or anyone uses are created by human beings and do not affect the idea they represent. Divine Mind, Immortal Mind, Christ Mind or Buddha Mind are all the same thing. Whether we call an affirmation a command, a plea or a prayer makes little difference in the operation of the Divine Law.

In meditation, it is not a question of our conscious mind dictating to the Divine Mind while asking the Divine Mind to do things that our mortal mind cannot do. We must consecrate (to make sacred) ourselves to the Divine Mind so that the process of meditation takes place. The purpose behind all of this is to make us masters of our fate.

Meditation should be silent because we cannot connect in meditation if we have a noisy mind. This is why we recommend concentration first. Concentration helps us gain control of the most unruly mind.

Meditation is the silent weighing of the answers we get to questions, or the silent waiting for the answers. When we meditate, we must block the mind of scattered thoughts – for the mind of the average person has many scattered thoughts per few seconds. But the mind must not be blank. The thought process should flow freshly. We need to bless and praise each thought as it enters into our consciousness. These answers given to us in meditation should relate to the question we place before the inner Self.

Psalm 119:15, **"I will meditate on your precepts, and fix my eyes on your ways."** The laws of God are so evasive, they must be meditated on and studied until our "eye is single" and we can really observe the works of God. Meditation brings with it the spiritual awareness of true understanding. Meditation will give us good judgment and free us from shame and error. We will achieve the Christ Mind and heal our entire cosmic structure.

Psalm 119:97, **"I will meditate upon your laws by day and night."** By meditation on God's precepts and laws, we obtain divine understanding and Illumination. Through working with the Illumination, we arrive at the point of finding the Self. Finding the Self is the quest of this course of study.

START WITH CONCENTRATION:

Pick an object in the room and look at it for ten minutes in full light.
Do this every day for four days during the week.
The next week do this for three days. The third week on Wednesday.
The fourth week, darken the room and concentrate on the same object with the light of three candles. Do this for five minutes every day for four days the first week; the second week, every day for three days; in the third week, two days during the week; and in the fourth week on Wednesday.

Then do this in the light and dark alternately, ten minutes in each, once a day for a week. This will establish the power of concentration. Meditation is then a retroactive function of concentration. It will carry us through. If we cannot concentrate, we will not be well balanced.

When starting meditation, pick a spiritual subject, unless there is a mundane problem. After entering into a spiritual attitude and forgetting all that is around you, set up the subject. Clear the mind, do not blank it, let it stay alive, but do not think. The thoughts that enter should be strictly related to your subject and should not be foreign to it. This will not work, however, if you have not learned concentration and have a fair mastery of it. Do not move on until successful the first time. Then you can meditate on other things.

Contemplation is a way of restrospecting what we have received and learned in meditation. Contemplation marks out a field of observation where we can bring the force of our concentration to bear on some topic.

AN EVERYDAY APPROACH:

1. Keep in mind before going to sleep that you will meditate before breakfast. Thus, you will be wide awake and obtain better results. This is also a good time to pray for something, as the mind is yet uncluttered with the day.

2. Get in the habit of thinking of God first. Then call on the Master Jesus or Mother Mary so that your consciousness will be immediately filled.

3. Consider it a sacred duty to practice the exercise of meditation daily. Try to use the same place and about the same time whenever meditating. Do not allow other things to interfere, if at all possible.

4. Body, soul and mind are to be trained simultaneously to gain the necessary spiritual balance.

5. Don't think of hastening spiritual development.

6. Do not criticize or condemn others. Keep your own doorstep clean.

7. Be kind, generous and tolerant of others, but be very exacting with yourself and your spiritual exercises. Live to your highest knowing.

8. Don't talk about your spiritual development except to your priest or teacher.

9. Spend as much time as possible with your spiritual work without shirking your daily duties. You are subject to habit. Once you are accustomed and feel the benefits of the cosmic contained in meditation, you will never be without it.

Patanjali, an Indian swami, defines meditation as "an unbroken flow of knowledge on a particular object." It is dwelling on one central idea, a diving down into the Self, the Divine Mind, for various associations connected with our question. This is fishing for the truth. Alchemists refer to meditation as "the fixation of the volatile." This means meditation has specific physical results changing the physical body of the person who meditates.

Meditation enables us to draw from within the right answer to every problem. We must not only have a problem but must admit to ourselves that the presence of the problem is an indication of our ignorance. This humbles us to accept the wisdom coming from the Self.

MEDITATION II

Meditation is the act of fishing in the subconscious or Divine Mind for answers. A fishhook makes us think of a line suspended in the universal spiritual water. We bait our hooks to induce the fish to bite. In other words, we want an answer or an experience of something, so we use striving and desire to expect light on our question. We must have a definite object in mind when we meditate. We have to suspend our conscious thought life in order to keep alert to the stirrings in the spiritual waters. Remember, the reason to meditate is to solve problems.

We must silence the superficial activity of our mind, just as a person fishing must sit quietly and patiently until the fish takes the hook. In Sanskrit writings, the suspension of thought that takes place in profound meditation is called "Samadhi." This leads to the revelation of the highest truths.

In meditation we keep the stream of consciousness flowing in relation to some particular object. In this way we gather impressions as things begin to reveal their solution to us. The process should be one of an active quest and not merely sitting passively, hoping for enlightenment. As we become proficient at meditation, we simply have to focus our attention on something, and the answers begin to unfold. Nature and God does not hide anything from us. It is our ignorance that veils our understanding and makes us think we are separate and mortal.

Begin the practice of daily meditation. Formulate your desires into specific problems. Focus the spotlight of your awareness on this and make every detail clear and definite. Do not try to imagine or sort through possible solutions. Watch the ideas that seem to rise up to the surface. Reject them unless they show some definite relation to the central purpose of your meditation. Keep the object always in view. At the end of a successful meditation, you will have received a revelation of some eternal principle that bears directly on your problem and presents you with a solution.

God has no problems and already knows all the answers. When we bait our hook in meditation, each bait has a particular attraction for a special fish in God's mind. Formulating the question clearly is baiting the hook. We have to be still until the fish takes the hook and we get some ideas.

When we are perfectly still in meditation, the spiritual centers of the body, the chakras, are synchronized and brought into balance. Purified and concentrated thought helps to attune these seven whirling centers of energy with the Cosmic Mind. Poise and balance are the consequence of this work. Perfect attunement and accord with nature are achieved because our stillness has allowed us to come into harmony with the rhythms and workings of God.

It is foolish and dangerous to concentrate or try to open or close these seven centers of energy without the guidance of a real spiritual teacher. For the average person, releasing these energies will produce a flood of power in the body that the person will not be able to control. This could easily throw the body out of balance and injure us. Avoid trick breathings. Just breathe in a relaxed way, quietly, rhythmically and deeply without huffing and puffing.

Do not grapple with a problem in meditation, just be mentally and physically still. If we are fishing, we don't have to always jiggle our hook or recast constantly. Keep still, as it might scare the fish away. Mental fussiness and physical itches scare the fish away, too. Don't be concerned about whether you are doing this correctly, just get out of the way and sit quietly in steady contemplation of the problem as you formulated it in your question.

When you get a bite, land your fish. Keep paper and pencil on hand and jot down things as you get them. Sometimes it will be a very long conversation with God. Many times you will not get what you expect because God sees the long view and has the truth that sets you free of your small view of life. We are fishing for a species of fish we have never seen and we don't know the answer. That's why we meditate. We will be amazed by the answers and how different our guesses really are from the truth.

One important reminder: Always set up your meditation with a prayer for guidance and protection so that you do not receive any negative influences that are not of God.

Look within for the answers, for the light, for the life and for the Self.

BLESSING I

A blessing is the movement of power, energy and life. It may be given either by the laying on of hands or by prayer. When giving a blessing, you must find out what the person needs. You make a mental image of that need. If you are with a person and you lay your hands on them, draw the power and life down within them to fill that form or image. Then the blessing has been accomplished.

When you bless someone who is not present with you, see the particular need of the person. Make a mental image of that need and fill that need within that person with power, force and energy. Then know that need has been fulfilled. Drawing the power and energy within that pattern gives life to that pattern so it will manifest.

There are many different types of blessings that fulfill our outward and inward needs. For example, when giving a blessing of strength, you see the person strong. You draw down the power, force, energy and life to that person. Your thinking of seeing her strong is what determines that blessing because it is through your thoughts that the pattern is set up to be filled. The pattern is you seeing the person strong. This makes the pattern. Then consciously drawing down the power, force, energy and life to someone is the fulfilling of the pattern, which will then manifest.

People in the religious field often say: "May the Lord bless you." The reality for this to take place is that you see it being done, and it is done. Giving a blessing is not just some religious jargon. It isn't just words. It is real! Things take place!

The real spiritual world is a world of movement – a world of action, real action and real movement. When Jesus laid his hands on a person and said: "Be blessed," they were really blessed in the highest sense. God gave all of us this function.

In order to give blessings, you must Know. We become the living link between God and human beings, bridging the connection with our thought and will. We become the bridge between heaven and earth, just as Jesus was.

The power of God is seen by seeing this world. This world we live in is real. It came about by God seeing this world and filling the form with power, force, energy and life. This is how this world came into existence. God's pattern and way of doing things is the way and pattern for us to do things.

If you know God is real, then you can give a real blessing. If God is a mental concept to you or some nice idea, please rethink everything because you will not be able to do anyone any good. Everyone should be a servant of God. Either you are serving God or you are serving you – yourself – and your petty little desires, which the Bible called "Beelzebub."

A priest is one whose whole life, inwardly and outwardly, is a conscious movement of service to God. A priest's whole life is a giving of blessings to people that brings the priest closer and closer to the Creator.

A realization of the presence of God is the most potent healing agency there is. One who realizes God inside and in others is a living vehicle for grace. Giving blessings to others requires that we have some love for people and that we desire to relieve their suffering and help them come back into balance, the way God made them.

Visualization is the art of mentally projecting a thought into the mind of God. Your thought is the form or the mold that God's substance will fill through the working of the Law. The power of your visualization is determined by the clarity of your image and the depth of your feeling and knowing. It depends on how much you are willing to put into it.

BLESSING II

In II Samuel 7:29, "Therefore now let it please You to bless the house of your servant, that it may continue forever before You; For You, Oh God, have spoken, and with your blessing let the house of your servant be blessed forever."

A blessing is an invested power and privilege given to creation by the Creator. With it comes the obligation to carry out the pattern and law of the Creator. To be blessed is to be joined together with the Creator as if God was the bridegroom and you, the bride. The blessing is a metaphysical and spiritual wedding. "Works is the way." Monks, nuns and priests receive this blessing at their ordination as they are blessed into service.

The divine Master requires our whole being in service for his honor and glory. Before the blessing is obtained, many conditions are required of the candidate. Usually the vows of Poverty, Chastity, Humility and Obedience are taken. The way of light is obtained in the blessings, beginning with the Humility vow. Humility is knowing that you know nothing and that without God you can accomplish nothing. When this blessing is realized, it will bring about a greater desire and acceptance of the blessing of Chastity.

Chastity is not a condition in which you are not married. It is a much deeper state of mind and soul than just not engaging in sexual activity. The fact of the matter is that many people who consider themselves to be married are not married. Legally, yes, by civil laws, they are and believe they are.

Chastity starts with our desires in respect to our thinking, our relationship to our Creator, and our desire to know God or Self. It is to have a close feeling to the Creator, the All-Encompassing One, the Elohim. The desire to know God above all other things makes us chaste of all base, selfish desires. This should come at the time of the blessing.

We may be married and still can strive for the blessing of Chastity, if both partners have given the other the freedom to seek the Self, and if each is considerate of the other's physical needs, because the physical sex act can, when performed in a whole way, be a balancing of forces and sharing of experiences. It is for the bearing of children – this is true, but it is also a fact that a state of unity exists in the Godly marriage.

Just being married is not Chastity. Many people look at the opposite sex and go through all the desires and emotions of sexual relations without ever knowing the other person. Actually, going through the physical sex is a very minor part of intercourse.

If we want to discipline ourselves for spiritual development and attainment, then abstaining will do fine. Sometimes abstaining when you are married is an avoidance of intimacy and should be examined. We are not advocating promiscuity in any form as it carries with it a karmic indebtedness. When Chastity has matured into full consciousness, it will create the desire to accept the blessing of Obedience, not to a person, place or thing, but to your own inner being, the Self. There are periods during your training when it is advisable to be obedient to the teacher you have accepted in order to spiritually advance. Obedience to the Creator is from within the Self.

I Chronicles 7:14, **"If my people, which are called by my name, humble themselves, and pray, and seek my face, and turn from their wicked ways, then I will hear from heaven and will forgive their sin, and will heal their land."** Healing is a blessing in this instance. The healing may transfer the power of the blessing to their land.

48

Humility, Chastity and Obedience create the virtue of Poverty. Poverty is also Humility, for we are speaking of paving the way to the power of the Spirit. A person can have a great deal materially and still manifest the blessing of Poverty. Jesus said to search first for the "Kingdom of Heaven" and that these things will be added to you.

When we have achieved spiritual Poverty, then Jesus, the Divine Son, will bless us in God's name, and to us will come the words of Jesus when He said, **"Blessed are the poor in spirit, for they shall see God."** When we say that Humility is Poverty, we are realizing the Divine Truth that those who are humble are truly poor in spirit. Humility and Poverty are in each other as the Father is in the Son.

Read Matthew 5, 6 and 7 for a better understanding of the teachings on divine blessing in the Sermon on the Mount. In Psalms it says, **"Blessed is the person that walks not in the counsel of the ungodly, nor stands in the way of sinners, nor sits in the seat of the scornful. For that person will be as a tree planted by the water; they will not be moved."**

When these blessings are obtained and incorporated, the disciple becomes the master and your faith will not waiver. They then become the Tree of Life and the Lamb of God. The blessed disciple who masters his life presents himself faultless before God's glory with exceeding joy. He will not falter but have a great victory. This blessing cannot be attained before the transformation of mind and brain. Set your affections on things eternal and prepare for the great blessing.

The key is in the words of Jesus, **"Lay not up for yourselves treasures on the earth, where moth and rust corrupt, and thieves break in and steal..."** Jesus says: **"For where your treasure is, there will your heart be also."** God will bless us if we will comply with God's Law and order.

49

Remember this one saying, and keep it in front of you at all times:

IF YOUR EYE BE SINGLE, YOUR WHOLE BODY WILL BE FULL OF LIGHT.

LIGHT I

People have written reams of words about light, yet they have failed to begin to delve into this subject. We have based all our work in studying the workings of the mind from a purely selfish standpoint. We have had the nerve to think that the mind was our personal possession. But we are learning the truth.

In studying the mind, we are studying the workings of the creative forces and energies of the universe existent within us. For generations, this is what we have called God, the mind out of which all things come and to which everything returns. To study the entire workings of this mind would take a lifetime, at least, and then we would only know how much, in reality, we did not know. We will study how we use or misuse this mind in relation to ourselves. This raises some questions: "Who am I? Where do I come from? And what is my function in this plane of manifestation?"

Consider this: Until we have seen the Self, or the God-being within us, we do not know our Self.

For over a million years, human beings have inhabited this plane. Although the earlier bodies were not as functional as our present form, the circumstances were different then. People lived very simply, consuming the plants and animals put there for their nourishment. There was joy and a long, peaceful life. There was no dis-ease, for in the simplicity of their own natures, they did not then, nor do we now, need to think. We need only to listen and follow the guidance from the inner Self.

But we are the problem children of the universe. We were given the power to create and to think, for in reality, our every thought is a creation in its own right. Once we began to think, we could no longer live in peace with those around us

51

because we began to think ourselves better than our neighbors. This was against our own nature. In the beginning, we lived in peace within ourselves and with God. We knew God and lived in complete faith that our every need would be provided for. We need to get back to this acceptance of Divine Providence. It is logical to assume that if our thinking caused all this dis-ease in the world, it should be simple enough to clean it up by our ceasing to think. This has been proven scientifically by some who have, for prolonged periods of time, studied people when they were resting comfortably. The metabolism of the body smooths out and a calm, peaceful air falls upon the room when we are not asleep but in a state of relaxation. To find our inner being, this is vitally important.

The ability to sit in a state of refined relaxation or rest allows the functions of the body to slow down. The process of thinking will stop. When you have really stopped the thinking process, look within. You have given up enough to let the light shine in. Then you can answer the age-old question of "Who am I?"

We are a cell in the mind of God. We have the opportunity to access all the intelligence in the mind that created us. By the grace of God, we have access to all the things of this plane, or any other plane, into which we might wish to look. In order to accomplish this, we must first find the inner Self. This is done by seeking the light. We don't mean the light of understanding, or the various other things people in their hypocrisy have called light. We mean just what is stated here – light!

Science calls this a pipe dream and refuses to acknowledge the Higher Self or the light. But they agree that when a person is quiet, there is an increase of light or energy around the body. They know there is a field of electrical impulses surrounding the body. Schools of enlightenment have known and taught for years that an aura exists around the human body. We sometimes call this our atmosphere. In reality, this is light.

By using our brain, we can control this flow of energy and light so that it is turned in rather than being continually cast out. But this can be done only by silencing the mind through which a vacuum is created to be filled with light.

There is a Law existent in the universe: "Nature abhors a vacuum." Thus, it is filled. In order to be assured that you will fill this vacuum with the pure light of Christ, it is necessary to cleanse the field of energy around the body of its negative and evil thoughts that emanate from within. To accomplish this, it takes one who can see the field and who knows what needs to be drawn out.

As stated in the beginning of this lesson, we came from the mind of the Creator. Therefore, we are but a part of this mind made manifest. This being so, we are but a thought pattern in that mind.

When we use the energy with which we are endowed to cleanse this pattern of all impurity – acquired by our lack of control in what filled that pattern – we will be in a constant state of Illumination. To attain this state of being, it is necessary to renounce the thinking, or not thinking, of those around us – to take conscious control of our atmosphere. We must keep out the thoughts that are not in accord with the workings of our being.

WE CONTROL OUR ATMOSPHERE ABSOLUTELY AND WITHOUT EXCEPTION.

Don't try this on your own. This is because you do not know yourself yet, nor do you know what your function is in regard to creation. And you will not know until you begin to work with God in peace and in understanding of the world around you by becoming that Self. Therefore, it is advisable for a seeker to take a teacher. This is one who does know, who has learned to control their personal atmosphere.

These beings live more in the spiritual world than in the flesh world, for they are in continual communion with the inner Self and with the forces of the universe. This is not to say that they are not in flesh bodies, because some of them are. It is possible to receive instruction from the higher planes through continual prayer and a conscientious striving to know. Often, though, these higher beings will merely guide you to a teacher on this plane, for they have their function on that plane to attend to also. Our first duty is to find this teacher. Then we must follow whatever instructions this teacher asks us to do bearing in mind at all times that if we knew the truth, we would not be seeking a teacher to guide us to our Illumination.

The things you are asked to do are not always things you think have anything to do with your Illumination at all. But then the teacher may smile and ask you to trust the process because they know what they are talking about.

Once you have cleansed your mind of thinking what everyone else is thinking, you must cleanse the body of the results of all that thinking. This is accomplished by eating a well-balanced diet and by continuing sound thinking. The most valuable thing to remember in this cleansing process is to keep the mind only on that which you are doing. Therefore, you must be doing something. Work! This is work on jobs of almost any kind that will tear your mind away from what you are learning, thereby letting these new teachings manifest in your being to replace that which you were thinking, causing you to need this teacher.

Once you have done this, you are ready to begin the process of looking within for the light. During all the preceding time, you have been learning to relax. Now you must learn to meditate.

54

Most teachers will tell you to meditate when you first go into training. But if you are honest with yourself now, you will admit that you were merely relaxing and often fell asleep instead of meditating. After a while of actual meditation, you will feel the influx of power that comes each time. What you are actually doing is letting go of your thinking entirely, thereby making yourself accessible to be filled with the light and the peace of God.

When you feel that power within you (and you cannot find a way to get away from it, as most people try to do) then finally just let go, and you will see the light. Then you will begin to know where you come from. As you begin to work with the power within you, the inner Self, you will know why you are here and what your function is.

LIGHT II

Light is the vehicle of life and life is the vehicle of Spirit. Light is life in action. The radiating force through the sun comes to us as light. It isn't light until it hits the substance of the sun. It becomes visible from the spiritual sun when it comes through the physical sun we see in the sky.

The veil of darkness is drawn to one side and destroyed in the Divine Light and Illumination of Christ. The Christ Light is the light that illumines everyone, bringing into focus the desires, thoughts and ideas of the Creator. The true light enlightens everyone who comes into the world. This light is the light of human beings.

Scientifically speaking, light is a form of radiant energy that acts upon the retina of the eye. Light transmits at about 186,000 miles per second by wavelength motion, or vibratory motion. This is its relative speed in its travel in our earth's atmosphere. This light is from the Sun of God, that which causes things to grow. Light moves at a very high rate of vibration.

The presence of light within and around the body is similar to a divine state which activates Illumination of a Christ state. It activates spiritual sight. It causes us to know, see and understand the things of God. Jesus said, **"You are the light of the world."** A city cannot be hidden, because of its light. Jesus is telling us that our spirituality is the very life of nature, that the light power of our magnetic structure demonstrates the power of God to all the universe. Being the light of the world, we must demonstrate the Christ to all beings. This is truly the light that enlightens everyone coming into the world.

Jesus said, **"If your eye be single, your whole body will be full of light."** This means that if all your vision, all your understanding, all your knowledge and devotion are one-

57

pointed on the spirit, then that great light of Christ will surround you with its loving power and keep you healthy and wise. The light is what regenerates the cells.

Practice seeing this light by using the knowledge given to you in the lessons on Meditation. Visualize light and let it soak into your body down to your toes.

In Paul's experience, Acts 9, it is recorded that suddenly a light flashed from heaven, he fell to the ground and was blind for three days. He immediately heard a voice. Paul had received the first degree of Illumination. His mind started to become spiritual, and he was now born of the light.

This light is what is needed in us; then all other things in our rate of vibration will begin to glow and grow. Light is issued forth from the Solar Ray and this is what gives life to the planet earth. In this way, God spiritualizes the earth through a perfect manifestation, human beings, who, in reality, are the image and likeness of the Creator, God.

In First John the message is given, **"We have heard from God and proclaim to you that God is light, and in God there is no darkness at all."** If we say we are in union with God and we walk in darkness, we lie and the truth is not in us. Walking in light is walking with God in that we are in tune with the Infinite Mind, our Father. The Word of Power, the spiritual Word, is our light and lamp. Psalm 119 states, **"Thy Word is a lamp for my feet, and light for my path."**

If we follow this light and become the children of the light, we will have communion one with another.   It is our purpose to help you find love, light and truth through the teachings of Jesus Christ and all masters and saints which are consistent with the teachings of all the world religions.

John concludes and so do we: **"And we know the Son of God has come and has given us understanding to know God** who is true, and we are in God who is true, in his Son, Jesus Christ." This is the true God and eternal life. So, find the light. Share it with humanity. Watch and pray.

Matthew 5: 14-16, **"You are the light of the world. A city built on a hilltop cannot be hidden. No one lights a lamp to put it under a bed; they put it on the lamp-stand where it shines for everyone in the house. In the same way your light must shine in the sight of people, so that, seeing your good works, they may give the praise to God in heaven."**

This lesson will give you some pointers on the way to Illumination. There is no exact process or method, no exact series of exercises that will work with every person in exactly the same order. Each person is different and has some different interval of development. If you will do what the Master Jesus taught, if you will be one-pointed, then you will come a long way. If your eye is single, your body will be full of light.

This is not a new thing or a new approach. This may be a little exhilarated in this Aquarian Age due to the fact that the energy around our earth has increased. This is the day of the New Heaven and the New Earth. Things that are not in accord with the teachings of Jesus Christ are being cleared away from the earth. People have been going through Illumination for thousands of years, even before the Master Jesus came, but then it was a long, rugged process.

We are very much privileged to have incarnated during this time because it is much simpler and easier to attain now than in the past. Seeking the light of Christ to come into your physical temple necessitates being under the direction of an intelligent teacher or highly evolved priest who can help you interpret what you are seeing and experiencing. You can thus be brought in contact with greater wisdom and receive some direct guidance. It is necessary that you be free from strong negative tendencies, drugs or alcohol. We expect that you have some control over your life and live an average life, at least.

You have to learn concentration. You learn control of mind by taking an object, such as an orange, something with life and color, and concentrating on it. Get quiet and relax with the object in front of you. Look at it and think about it. Think about its parts, how it grew, about its color, its texture, what it is composed of. Think of the plant or tree it grew from, how it grows, and how it attaches to the earth. This same power, life and light is what we are seeking to attain within our own physical body. If you can think of these things for a few minutes, thinking about this one thing only, without letting outside thoughts in, then you have started to learn to control your mind and thinking. It takes varying lengths of time to accomplish this. The effort put into this is the keynote to all spiritual revelation and reality.

Next, we have to learn to visualize things, even objects that are not present. It should involve the re-creation within the mind of the colors and life-like reality of its existence.

Then you will learn meditation. This is not quietly doing nothing, sitting blankly. Nor is it letting strange and foreign thoughts come in, or allowing visitations from another world to take control and run rampant with your thinking. Meditation is a distinct tool of the mystics. Meditation is learning how to contact and make yourself available to the inner wisdom within the mind of God.

You learn how to be perfectly quiet and lose all consciousness of the body. Then you think of the question or the subject that you want to meditate on. You think about how this information will pertain to you and what you want. You ask an intelligent question, being careful to frame it just right before you go into meditation. Ask this mentally or vocally, then clear your mind, letting the mind stay alive. Then, in a few minutes, you should get thoughts about your question or topic. If you get thoughts on other topics, you do not have enough control and should begin again by clearing the mind and getting quiet. If the foreign, unrelated stuff continues, then abandon the meditation for a short period of time before repeating it. Then you can start to persist in realizing the Christ light within you.

There are twelve great Solar Initiations, but only nine on the physical level. Birth, walking, talking, reasoning, puberty, leaving home, marriage, having children, Baptism, Illumination, Self-Realization and finally Death or Ascension. In our passage through life we might only go through some of them. Maybe we will spend a whole life attaining part of one. Now, in this school, we will experience most of them. The power of God moving through the Master Jesus Christ will motivate these experiences, and we will attain them as experience.

EXERCISE: Visualize an egg of light around you as you sit in meditation. Let that light soak into your cells and fill every part of you. Do this for fifteen minutes each day.

Matthew 6: 22-23 **"The light of the body is the eye. If therefore your eye is single, your whole body will be filled with light. But if your eye is diseased, your whole body will be all darkness. If then the light that is inside you is darkness, what darkness that will be."**

Matthew 11:30 **"My yoke is easy and my burden is light."**

Matthew 17:2 **"There in their presence, He was transfigured: his face shone like the sun and his clothes became as white as the light."**

Luke 11:35 **"See to it then that the light inside you is not darkness. If, therefore, your whole body is filled with light, and no trace of darkness, it will be light entirely, as when the lamp shines on you with its rays."**

Luke 16:8 **"For the children of this world are more astute in dealing with their own kind than are the children of light."**

The darkness shows up when the light increases, and we must rid ourselves of it. As a group of people form a consciousness over a city or country that we call mass mind, the Christ Light emanating from the spiritual sun gets filtered through this mass mind. This sometimes appears as a deep gray. In the morning it is somewhat cleared up and purified. The outer atmosphere is very deep blue, not for lack of light, but because there is no resistance. The finer the light, the more penetrating it is.

When things look the bleakest, the radiant light is close by. The darkest hour is just before the dawn. When the sediment of our misthinking is removed and our sight is clear, then there will be nothing to resist the light. Only the prepared soul can bear the intensity of the light.

John 1:4-9 **"All that came to be had life in Him and that life was the light of human beings, a light that shines in the dark, a light that darkness could not overpower. A man came, sent by God. His name was John. He came as a witness to speak for the light, so that everyone might believe through Him. He was not that light, only a witness to speak for the light. The Word was the true light that enlightens everyone; and He was coming into the world."**

John 3:19-21 **"On these grounds is the sentence pronounced: that though the light has come into the world, men have shown they prefer darkness to the light** because their deeds were evil. Indeed, everybody who does wrong, hates the light and avoids it, for fear his actions should be exposed; but the person who lives by the truth comes out into the light, so that it may be plainly seen that what he does is done in God."

John 5:35-36 "**John was a lamp alight and shining, and for a time you were content to enjoy the light that he gave.**"

John 8:12 "**When Jesus spoke to the people, He said: I am the light of the world, anyone who follows Me will not be walking in the dark; he will have the light of life.**"

John 12:35-36 "**The light will be with you only a little longer now. Walk while you have the light or the dark will overtake you. You who walk in the dark do not know where you are going. While you still have the light, believe in the light and you will become the sons and daughters of light.**"

Ephesians 5:8 "**You were darkness once, but now you are light in the Lord; be like children of light, for the effects of the light are seen in complete goodness and right living and truth.**"

Hebrews 10:32 "**You must never forget those days past when you had received the light and went through such a great struggle.**"

LIFE

To most people, life is a combination of experiences that lead to an understanding of other people and places. To a carpenter, life would consist of him getting up at a certain time, eating, going to the job, going home in the evening, eating dinner and then having an evening of TV or something of that sort. In reality this isn't life at all. This is his understanding of what life is.

Life is the movement of power within your body. Life is a force and not concepts or understanding. We can define life as an animating force, a source of vitality.

Jesus said if you lose your life you shall have eternal life. When we give up our ideas of having our personal understanding of things, our personal time, we let it all go and give ourselves over totally to the Creator, then we will feel the surge of power run through our whole being. Then we will live of the Creator.

The great Christ, the Son (Sun) of God, is the source of all life. The Christ gives life to the animal kingdom, the vegetable kingdom and to human beings. Plants definitely have life, for they grow and propagate, but they do not think. They do not build their own mental concepts. So life is not a mental concept. It is a living, moving, dynamic power running through our bodies without thought, without concept.

Our opinions get us into the biggest trouble, for we will, with our half-blinded physical eyes, see the world and proclaim our opinion on things we only half see. Then we will label these things as scientific facts.

Life is universal because it has one great Source; therefore all things that contain life are linked together. When we let go of our opinions of race, creed and color and look into another person without labeling them with our biases or narrow-mindedness, we will begin to see the way things really are. We will take people just the way they are, and we will feel, see and know that we are not separate as it may appear. It doesn't mean we are them and they are us, but the one life knits each of us together through the Christ.

John 10:9 **"I am the door; by Me if anyone enters in, they shall be saved, and shall go in and out and find pasture. But the thief comes to steal, to kill and to destroy; I am come that they might have life, and that they might have it more abundantly."**

The great Christ permeates the earth with light, life and love through the Lord Jesus. Jesus Christ and Mother Mary are the channels of life for the earth. We must become conscious of this reality, for until we do, we will remain dead. In the New Testament, Jesus talked about the living dead. These are people who walk and think but who have not the power of the Christ running through their bodies. For it is this power that regenerates our physical body.

Due to the lack of life force, we are plagued by dis-ease and deterioration of the physical body. If we know God and Jesus, we will have the life force running through our body continually, which will keep us healthy and wise. The teachings of Jesus are real, and those who follow Him will experience a regeneration of the physical body that will not be breaking down all the time.

> Life is the force of the Spirit.
> Life is the divine emanation.
> Life is God in action.

Genesis 2:7 says, **"Then God formed the human out of the dust from the ground and breathed into his nostrils the breath of life, and man became a living being."** The Creator gives each creature this divine emanation to prove God's existence and manifestation. It is through life that the Word becomes manifest in flesh and dwells among us. Life has three stages as does every other facet of spiritual existence: Formation, growth and perfection.

The Creator formed humankind from the dust of the earth. The dust symbolizes the unmanifested Word of God, or Idea. The Creator forms the idea in universal mind. The unmanifested and the dust are one and the same thing. They are all form – the first stage of formation.

The breath of God is Spirit. It is the office of the breath of God as Spirit to create a pattern that can be filled. Once a pattern is created, we enter into life – and become a living soul – and the stage of growth is accomplished.

Genesis goes on to say that God planted a garden in Eden. There, God put the human being that was formed. Eden represents Nirvana – the highest state of universal Mind. The garden represents our heavenly existence, our life in that state of mind. Genesis tells us that God made to grow every tree that is pleasant to sight and good for food. Trees represent the many ways of life our individual manifestations can express. Genesis goes on to say that these many expressions were pleasant and good. This means that all the expressions of life are to be visualized and partaken of, each in accord with our desire.

Genesis tells us that the Tree of Life is there, symbolizing the mainstream of existence – the unlimited source of pure Spirit, the Truth, the Self. The Tree of Knowledge of good and evil also grew there, representing duality. The Tree of Knowledge of good and evil was purely symbolic; it was male and female.

We had only arrived at the stage of growth, and we were unable to eat of this fruit in this state of mind – the state we were in at the time of the Garden incident. Therefore God forbade us to be so tempted by the serpentine force of uncontrollable desire to attain. We violated the Law of nature and unnaturally created a false image of ourselves, because we had not grown to perfection and attained mastery. We were unable to control our creation, and this was the original sin.

In this age of the Lord of Life and the great Christ power, we are growing to perfection and are now ready to dominate life. We stand at the threshold of pure life, not bound by handicap, inhibition or fear. We walk in the liberty of the Christ, and demonstrate the truth that makes us free. There is a river in Eden that waters the Garden. This river is the spiritual life that waters the highest state of mind in which God dwells. The river was divided into four, plus the original river equals five. This symbolizes the five portals of sense in human beings and the four elements of creation, plus the fifth, which is the spiritual or the quintessence.

Gold was also introduced into the Garden. Gold is the materialization of God's pure idea. Gold symbolically represents the real you when the alchemist states that they turn base metals into Gold. We are forming ourselves out of the dust of the earth, making ourselves a living soul. We are being transferred out of darkness into light. **"In Him was life, and the life was the light of men. The light shines in the darkness and the darkness has not overcome it."**

The Creator has formed the Golden Force of God, the divine son and daughter that becomes the life of the world. The Sun Mediators become the power that brings forth many other sons and daughters through right understanding of the Self and the oneness with life. There is only one life and one Self, the primordial force for good. This primary force is infinitely indwelling, full of divine wisdom and knowledge. It is incapable of transgressing the Law, for the Law is part of its nature.

Jesus Christ was the first begotten of many divine sons and daughters of God. It was said, "in Him was life..." He is a personification of divine life. He transmitted that life to us through the divine bloodstream of Spirit. This is why, in John 1:7, it says, **"He came for testimony, to bear witness to the light, that all might believe through Him."** The blood of Jesus Christ is the divine life of Spirit, not any of the denser forces. His life was incapable of sin. Therefore we to whom this life is imparted are also free from sin because we are partakers of his blood and his life.

John 10:10 **"The thief comes only to steal and kill and destroy. I came that they may have life, and have it abundantly."** Let us not forget that we are partakers of the Father's divine love. As we are anointed with water and spirit, we partake of this new life.

Using the Law, let us move forward and grow in perfection. Let us stand fast in that liberty wherewith Christ has set us free. Otherwise that liberty is divine life in a yoke of bondage. For those yokes of bondage are, in reality, false ideas and images created by the only devil that actually exists – mass mind.

The center of life is neither in thought nor in feeling nor in will, nor even in consciousness, so far as it thinks, feels or wishes. For real truth may have been penetrated by a person and possessed in all these ways, and escaped us still. Deeper even than consciousness, there is being itself, our very substance, our nature. Only those truths that have come from this region of being itself are lasting and real.

LOVE

Love is a source of power, though love of itself has no power. Love is the reciprocal action of give and take. Love creates a vacuum that necessitates reaction. Remember, nature abhors a vacuum, but nature does not repel love. The Law says that if we love, we must be loved. Love begets love.

Love is a part of the Law that runs the universe. It is a divine attribute, having its origin in the act of creation. The creation must automatically manifest it, since the creation is nothing more than the materialized substance of the Creator. Love is the generator of the Law. Therefore, truth says divine love always does and always will supply our every need. (The etymology of the word "need" means death, or to be exhausted). Love is functional in that it responds to the Law. The etymology of the word "love" means "approval." So we could read total acceptance in the word "love."

God encompasses the Universe and fills it with a substance we can call love. Just as a good mother or father throws a loving blanket of support, encouragement and protection over a child, the Father holds each being in conscious, thoughtful embrace. This is love. God's love is the Supreme Love; our love for God is a reflection of that love. Our love for each other is the principle of divine love made active and manifest.

If we love someone, we don't worry about trust. Taking possession drives us from what we love, because there is no flow, yin and yang. The only flow would be from us to it, as will. This would cut love off. Let our love be in deed, and not word only. Love is doing, performing daily acts.

It is hypocrisy to talk about love and yet refuse to move over a little to make room for another person, or to let those who depend on you go without your attention, or to ignore the needs of others. If we can't see the needs of those closest to

71

us, how can we discern the need of the world at large and cure them? Love is knowing someone's predicament and doing something about it. Love thinks ahead and gives an encouraging word where it is needed. Love consists in not hurting anyone in the first place.

Love and hate are very similar because we have to be attached by attraction to love or to hate. Love and fear are opposites and cannot exist together. Fear causes adrenaline to increase. That is like a state of shock, and therefore, we are not relaxed. Love must be relaxed to flow. Love is the river of life that flows from the throne of God. Without love, we cannot see God. For we have to reach to God with love to see the Creator. The Creator functions through love action; so it is the love aspect of the heart that helps us see God in another person and finally in ourselves. Love is not an emotion – it is an eternal truth. Love is a total, unconditioned acceptance, unfailing constancy and support.

Psalms 31:23 **"Love God, all you saints of God. The Creator preserves the faithful, but abundantly requites those who act haughtily."** It is God who preserves us. Hebrews 12:6 **"For whom God loves, God chastens, and scourges every person whom God receives."**

John 15:17 **"Greater love has no one than this, than to lay down your life for your friends."** In loving another, we love God who is present in everyone. Love necessitates giving and sharing without hope of reward.

John 3:16 **"For God so loved the world that God gave God's only Son, that whoever believed in Him should not perish, but have eternal life."**

John 4:19 **"We love, because God first loved us."** We see that our love is the result of God's love, and the manifestation of all our love is nothing more than the effect of God loving all of creation.

I John 4:16-20 **"God is love; and you who dwell in love dwells in God, and God in you... In love there can be no fear, but fear is driven out by perfect love; because to fear is to expect punishment, and anyone who is afraid is still imperfect in love. We are to love, because God loved us first. Anyone who says, 'I love God' and hates a sister or brother is a liar, since a person who does not love the sister or brother that they can see cannot love God, whom they have never seen."**

I Corinthians 13:4-8 **"Love suffers long and is kind; love envies not; love is never boastful, is not puffed up, does not behave itself unseemly, seeks not her own, is not easily provoked, thinks no evil; Love rejoices not in iniquity, but rejoices in the truth; bears all things, believes all things, hopes all things, endures all things. Love never fails."**

Love of the creation gives us knowledge of the creation. Love of others gives us knowledge of others. It is spiritually correct to say that we cannot know anything without loving it. Love restrains us from doing damage to God's creation. Love is a thermostat that keeps our vehicle of expression well under control. Let us pray for love, let us seek love, and when we receive it, let us exercise it and hold fast to it. For it is a precious stone, a valuable part of our functioning here.

Jesus said in John 15:5 **"As the Father has loved Me, so have I loved you; abide in my love."** Jesus loved us in the same way and with the same respect that God loved us. This is the secret of true loving.

The Creator creates the creation, and in turn, the creation continually recreates the Creator. This is the Father having divine activity of give and take within its own androgynous being. This is love expressed cosmically.

The Pharisees asked Jesus what was the greatest commandment of all, and He said, **"You must love God with all your heart, with all your soul, and with all your mind. This is the greatest and first commandment. The second resembles it: You must love your neighbor as yourself. On these two commandments hang the whole Law, and the Prophets also."** Matthew 22:34-40

Matthew 5:44-45 **"But I say to you, love your enemies, bless them that curse you, do good to them that hate you, and pray for them that spitefully use you, and persecute you. For if you love those who love you, what reward have you? Do not even the publicans do the same?"**

John 14:15-21 **"If you love Me, keep my commandments. If you have my commandments and keep them, it is you who love Me; and you who love Me shall be loved of my Father, and I will love you, and will manifest myself to you."**

SPIRITUAL BODY I

The spiritual body is the most important of our vehicles of expression. The preparation of the spiritual body allows for the coming of the Christ light into our dense physical body.

I Corinthians 15:42-46:
"So it is with the resurrection of the dead. What is sown is perishable, but what is raised is imperishable. It is sown in dishonor, it is raised in glory. It is sown in weakness, it is raised in power. It is sown a physical body, it is raised a spiritual body. If there is a physical body, there is also a spiritual body. Thus it is written, 'The first man Adam became a living being; the last Adam became a life-giving spirit.' But it is not the spiritual which is first, but the physical, and then the spiritual. The first person was from the earth, a person of dust; the second person is from heaven. As was the person of dust, so are those who are of dust; and as is the person of heaven, so are those who are of heaven. And we, who have been modeled on the earthly person, will be modeled on the heavenly person."
We call the spiritual body the primary body, because it is the body that holds the visible, physical and chemical matter together. This gives us our visible human form. The spiritual body is the cover of the spark of life or Self.

We have three bodies: Physical, Spiritual and the Soul that is around the Self. These are referred to in the Bible as the terrestrial, celestial and mental bodies.

As the Spiritual Body descends and accepts the cosmic energy, it increases in density and intensity. The divine spark within it begins to evolve and the memory of the soul starts taking on the form of the physical body as it approaches physical birth or incarnation. As the spiritual body evolves and the power of the sun, the Christ, is accepted into it, it enlarges and becomes less dense. The spiritual body goes through the same stages of formation and growth that all forms go through. The circle with the dot in the center is the symbolic representation of the spiritual body. The dot within the circle represents the divine spark or Self. The circle around it is the emanation, the life-giving spirit or the lost atom. This is the understanding of Adam and atom. One is scientific, one is spiritual. Scriptures declare the last Adam to be Jesus Christ, who represents the divinity in human beings.

Paul says in Corinthians 15:51-52, **"Listen, I tell you a mystery. We shall not all sleep, but we shall all be changed, in a moment, in the twinkling of an eye, at the last trumpet."** We are being changed in the twinkling of an eye, and the realization starts with the spiritual body.

The divine spark, Logos, called by the mystics "Fiat," burns its way through the spiritual body and removes all dross until it amalgamates itself with it. The spark of life and the body become one. When this happens on an individual level, we say that the Self is found, because the seeing consciousness of the vehicles permits us to actually see the Self and the radiant being. The finding of the Self is what the scriptures declare as the great awakening.

Through the spiritual body our perishable nature becomes the imperishable nature of God. So Paul says the corruption must put on incorruption, because this is an immutable law of the spiritual body. Each of the three bodies has their own laws functioning within them but are consistent with the Law of Cause and Effect.

The first man, Adam, was like the awakening, only in a state of formation. The body could only contain some of the divine spark and its emanation. So we have, allegorically, the fall of Adam.

The spiritual body has the ability to attune itself with other bodies and make itself one with them. It is important to remember that God gives us the body we need. What God chooses we call Karma, for it is the effectual reaction of the Law of Cause and Effect. We call it God's choice, because God is the basic or causeless Cause.

In the New Testament it states that Christ shall be made alive and that a quickening of the Spirit shall take place. This is made possible only through the spiritual body. Thus, in each incarnation the spiritual body grows stronger, and the spiritual body provides food for the inward growth and for the other bodies, making them interdependent on each other. The spiritual body is responsible for the care of all things contained in all three bodies.

Study I Corinthians 15 so you will understand the Mysteries of Christ.

When we use the word "spiritual body," we are talking about an electrical matrix that really exists, even though most of us do not see it with our physical eyes. But there are many things in science and medicine that demonstrate the existence of the spiritual body and its working through the physical body. In various forms of healing, the physical body often makes its greatest recovery **after** therapy has been stopped. This shows there is some agent other than the applied therapy functioning in order to bring this about. There is an intelligent force and pattern working upon the diseased part needing the healing.

The Self lies within the spiritual body and reflects through the physical. We must begin with the God Self. Around the Self is the soul and in it is the record of the soul memory as we travel from life to life. We know how to improve and change conditions in the physical body so that we may adapt to the conditions of the physical world into which we are incarnating. The Self and soul is the eternal that we are and always will be.

We must begin in the innermost core of our being. This is the Infinite God who is at the core of each one of us. When we have attained the consciousness and gained the divine rights, raised ourselves and our vehicles to that level of reality, then we will be functioning at the level of God Realization. Then we can really conform to the First Commandment to love the Lord God with all your heart, with all your soul and all your mind.

The soul, or sheath around the Self, collects the impressions of energy from the blood, its vibration, which fills in with our emotions and actions and leaves their karmic record in the soul. The soul is that which carries the form and pattern in our future life. This is impinged on the negative pole of the Self. The Self is a cell in the body of God and shines forth in the physical vehicle to everything around it. Every organ we find in the physical body reveals its strength and perfection of function, and may tell us how closely we are manifesting the rhythm and basic form of the body that God had in mind.

When we have a weakness or imperfection in an organ or part of the physical body, it is telling us that in some way in the past we may have broken down through misuse of this organ. Perhaps we never gained mastery over the body or even tried to separate ourselves from the basic form of the creation of God, cutting off the life force and reality of our spiritual body. The spiritual body is also called the vital body, the causal body, the astral body. It's all the same thing.

When an organ is not functioning properly, the potential normal electrical strength of the spiritual body has broken down, and so the molecules and cells are not functioning intelligently according to the form of the spiritual body. For example, if the liver is functioning poorly and we are not assimilating food properly, then the liver in the spiritual body and the psychic stuff from which it is made does not have the electrical strength to cause the physical organ to take care of the normal functions.

When a person receives the light of Christ or Illumination, really, the spiritual body becomes charged up. This explains why, if we have any physical infirmities, they will show up. This is why we call down the light or Spirit upon the student when she has physical infirmities and this will increase the potential of the physical body where it is, in this undercharged state. When the organs are brought up to charge, then any foreign pathology, infection or growth will be immediately drawn out and destroyed because they are not part of the basic pattern of the spiritual body. They will be broken up into electron particles and radiated out. The cells will reorganize themselves to reflect the perfect pattern of the spiritual body and reabsorb the spiritual body's intelligence.

Sentient energy working through the spiritual body knows how each organ is supposed to function. The reflex systems of nerves are merely reflections of those in the spiritual body. The true memory and intelligent operation of the physical body as a whole is governed by the mind of the soul. A healing takes place when the physical and spiritual body function perfectly according to the soul pattern.

Violations of the Ten Commandments or the two great Commandments of Jesus, things like evil, destructiveness and selfishness, create a lower frequency of vibration. These actions crystallize the density of the soul energy and do not permit the passing of power, light and cosmic energy from the Self, which is of God. Some light passes, but not in its purer state. This can cause a premature aging process.

The Master Jesus promised us eternal life. We can have perpetual life regardless of whether we mean a physical or a spiritual state. It would not be in one state and not in the other. When we try to divide the physical from the spiritual, we are not having eternal life. All vibration and energy passes through our atmosphere, but not all comes in a pure state. This emanates into the body and is not correctly in harmony with the perfect creation of the spiritual body. Thus we may experience disease.

Our fears can cause illness. These can manifest physically and soon become a pattern in our individuality.

SPIRITUAL BODY II

We are talking about the spiritual body and relating it to the function of the soul and how to maintain the physical body. The emotions carry vibrations resulting from our acts and deeds that often cloud and crystallize, to a certain extent, the peripheral area of our soul. The soul determines our future life pattern. The soul is the negative pole to the Self. The clarity of the God force shining through from the Self is determined by the density and vibration of the soul. Our experiences in life are impinged on the negative pole of the Self, and they determine what shines forth and comes through the soul. The good, positive things flow more perfectly, smoothly and harmoniously, manifesting in the physical body.

The spiritual body is never affected by disease in any way. It is not affected by any accident or problem we have. The spiritual body has every organ, cell and tissue in it, in a colorless perfect form that we have in the physical body. Some of the life force and the solar forces manifest directly in the physical, but we can use natural healing to bring them into balance. Each organ represents a different aspect of creation. Digestion represents assimilation, as an example.

When we have a disease, like arthritis, it can be because of the negation or state of mind we have. We may be consciously or unconsciously blocking the radiation from the Self that is seated primarily in the spiritual body. The spiritual body sends its energies in trying to maintain health in the organ affected or the place of impairment trying to maintain the chemical balance in the physical body. The physician will say, "You have arthritis," or cancer or whatever. In such cases, there can be a pathological deposit forming in the body, and the perfect physical form is distorted.

Not all disease or illness may be caused by our actions and thinking. Jesus was asked by the Pharisees whether the blind man sinned to cause his illness or his parents sinned. His answer was that God would be glorified by his condition and that he had been born blind simply to be one of the ones cured by Jesus to give glory to God. We need to not judge and be compassionate for the sufferings of others, since we do not know whether they are working out some karmic condition or have thought amiss. Some conditions are primarily from environmental toxins that everyone is responsible for. Treat each condition of the body as a teacher instructing you what needs to be done.

The Self lies in the spiritual body, but it is also dimensionally seeable in the physical. The person taking on the aspects of Christ is beginning to assume and take on the aspects of the Lord of the Sun and is learning to not impair in any way the perfect flow of the life force and healing forces of the Christos.

Sometimes an illness is really an elimination or cold process sloughing off negative stuff. It is not necessarily disease. It does demonstrate a powerful healing force of the Christ that is eliminating negative material from the body as well as foreign things we pick up in foods that are not adaptable to the body. Water pollution and poisons in the air we breathe can clog the eliminative processes.

Once we have been exposed to the basic laws and principles of creation, we may perfect our own universe. When we learn to use our God-given tools, we can detect and screen out all harmful substances from our bodies and atmosphere. As we become more like Christ, we will not need as great a quantity of food and thus we will be exposed to less impurity. Our relationship to the Christ force will minimize the flow of negative forces into our bodies. We will have reached the condition that an old hymn called: "resting in the arms of God." Then we will truly be letting go and letting God.

The psychic body is not a true body or a distinct physical substance. It is highly effluvious and reactive to emotions and sound. Light has a powerful effect on this substance as it causes it to become more one and less reactive, because the light of the sun is uniform and not different in any substance whether here or there, or in one organ or another of the body. The psychic body is a mediator between the physical and the spiritual. It is a borderline state much like the term "limbo." The psychic world is an intermediary state between the dense world and the lower heaven world. These lower states of vibration are part of God's creation and it is the substance that motivates and gives us the form of the spiritual body in its lower form. The psychic body can be used as a reflecting substance to teleport images and figures of a higher state to earth and our other five senses. It is mostly a negative force, potentially, in that it is a step down from the spiritual body. It is the flesh of the spiritual body.

We can be masters of the elements in our body and thus become masters of our spiritual attainment through the power of God manifest in the light of Christ in our being. Let's not sell short the spiritual function and control of the psychic body, and the magnificence of its creation. Its simplicity of operation is as enthralling as it appears to be mysterious. Yet without drugs or knife, the psychic physician can perform healing and surgery as an instrument of God.

In this age, we can now become brothers and sisters with Christ.

The electrical structure of the spiritual body sends its energy through the physical. The higher frequencies activate and feed the physical even though invisible to our physical eyes. Some scientists have formulated complicated theories about the radiations from the physical. The human body contains approximately 140 grams of potassium, causing the emission of some 80,000 body particles per second. These tiny body particles permeate through all parts of our bodies at a tremendous speed.

There is electrical nerve energy in the body which, when fired by the brain or some reaction, causes a stimulus along a nerve to contract the muscles of the body. These nerves transfer electrical impulses in vibratory form from place to place in the body. There are certain places where this energy manifests its strength. The energy flows hard and escapes in the nerve terminals. The hands and the head appear to be the principal terminals for electrical nerve energy. The tips of the fingers have long been used by mystics and healers as terminal points of radiation.

SOUL I

The soul is the shell of the Self, that which protects the Self from all interference. Psalms 42:2 **"My soul thirsts for God, for the living God. When shall I come and behold the face of God?"**

The soul is related to the emotional body and affects it through development, thirsting after God. This unfolds the soul and reveals it to us. Judges 5:21 **"March on, my Soul, with might."** As the soul marches forward, the Self advances. The soul produces intense protections for the Self.

There are spiritual qualities within the soul that bring about almost instantaneous Illumination when the outer ego lets go and lets God. We develop soul through meditation and study of the New Testament.

In Revelation we find that the Way which is seen preserved is the soul or sheath of the Self, because here is stored the record of past lives. The Self, encompassed by the soul, is the cell or body of God. Its ever-effulgent revelations carry with it the universal knowledge of the existence of the Way, for it was God's creation. We ask about the immortality of the soul and the employments of heaven and our relationship with these. We will not have a satisfactory answer until we have reached through the Self to the Akashic records, or the mind of the Creator.

Revelation 20:4 **"Then I saw thrones, and seated on them were those to whom judgment was committed. Also I saw the souls of them that were beheaded for the witness of Jesus, and for the Word of God, and which had not worshipped the beast, or its image and had not received its mark on their foreheads or their hands. They came to life and reigned with Christ a thousand years."**

Unless the soul is maintained by prayer, meditation and Bible study, the Self cannot find Illumination or Realization. Its potential must be activated by thought. All material endeavors must be put to one side until the soul is enriched to the point where it begins to expand its activity of life. Then the Self will be Realized and Illumined and found through the enriching of the soul. This is because the soul functions on the plane of the heaven world.

Ezekiel 18:4 **"Behold all souls are mine; the Soul of the Father, as well as the soul of the Son is mine; the soul that sins shall die."**

Psalm 33 **"Our soul waits for God."**

The Creator, God, is a consuming fire. The soul waits for that fire to burn out the dross, then elevates itself, and the Self is realized. All power is contained in the soul that has realized the Self because its Karma is paid off.

The great soul force is infinite, indestructible and has a very high rate of vibration. The soul came into the human body at birth; it leaves it at so-called death. Before it came into the body, this soul substance existed somewhere and manifested in some nature. When it leaves the body, it does not die. It cannot cease to exist; it is immortal. It cannot remain on the earth plane without a vessel or vehicle to inhabit. It has to have a material manifestation to be on earth. So, it must return to its original source.

During its temporary residence in a human body, the soul stays in touch with the divine source from which the soul emerged and to which it returns. All souls on the earth, like all souls in the cosmic plane, are in constant attunement with all other souls. Tests have been done to show that the minds and intelligences of departed souls can communicate with the minds of souls here on earth. This is because one soul is attuned with all other souls. Thought vibration operates great distances and makes possible mental telepathy or mind-reading.

The subconscious mind is the mind of the soul. Music is God's language of the soul. The difference in the expression of my soul versus others' makes up my personality. Individuality is a material manifestation of earth habits and life.

There is that part of the soul that makes it a soul. We cannot say it is this or that, but it is a quality that is much like grace. It is that which is above the soul essence itself. It is simple. It is impressionable. It is pure nothing, yet it is the ALL – the totality of our life. There is no name for it – this pure nothing – unknown and yet closer than breath. We can call it receptive power, this divinity of ours. It is the uncreated light of the Christos.

This is the Absolute – free from all name – and is all that there is in our life now. It is pure God with our life representation coloring it. This body of soul is above love, higher than grace and knowledge, for these are distinguishable.

It is in this receptive power that God does blossom and flourish with the Master Jesus and Mother Mary. Its actions are visible in the dense world. It is through God's power that the creating God brings forth the only-begotten Son, the Christos, the essential part of itself, and in the light of this is cast the shadow of the Holy Ghost.

Peace be with you.

SOUL II

Soul – what is it? The soul does not have such a material nature that we can hope to sense it just by looking at it alone. This is part of the job of the teacher. It is there, the Self and soul. It is part of our objective and subjective work. We seek to bring each person, at their wish, into the realization of the Self. Therefore, the teacher touches on the sense of soul.

We have a material body and a spiritual body. We have a soul. The blood contains what is not seen or perceived objectively because it is not visible objectively. We know that the blood contains plasma containing white and red corpuscles. It is the medium for carrying the real power and energy of the Christ and the light.

We can see the Self. This can be done. We will notice that there is a soul, for it is around the Self. We can understand it and learn to work with it through its manifestations. We can see it. The manifestations are so definite that we cannot make any mistake about its presence. Just as we can define the things that belong to our hearts, we can also define those things that belong to the soul. It has a unique function that does not have to do with any other part of our existence. The soul and the Self, this is you.

As one mystic put it, if we had never been told and never heard about the existence of the soul, our studies, our lives and our observations would have forced us to create or invent a soul to explain what we had observed.

The Creator created human beings out of the dust of the earth, breathed into their nostrils the breath of life, and they became a living soul. We take this statement literally. Our material body is of the negative elements of the earth. Our body is made of dust. It is like the clay images molded as some of the gods. It is like a pot in the potter's hands. For it is that which is in our hands which we mold and shape as we go along.

Compare the lifeless body of a person with someone who is lying beside it, asleep. What is the difference? They seem outwardly similar. They both have the same physical and spiritual organs and seem a replica of the other. The spiritual essence is there in the one as life force, not in the other. In one there is breath, in the other not. In the one, something is still present, while it is absent in the other. Our conclusion is that the soul is absent in the lifeless body. The soul travels from life to life.

There is a close relationship between breath and the psychic aura, between the breath and the psychic body, and the spiritual body and its charging. In the Zend Vesta, the language of the Atlanteans, and then in Sanskrit, Greek and Latin, there is a relation between breath and soul. The word "soul" and "breath" have the same root and are synonymous. But there was a distinction between soul and spirit. The ancients knew the functions that the soul and breath maintained in our existence. Some said that the divine principle or First Cause was from the breath of God that permeates all things. This breath manifested in the creative laws and matter which we term "spirit." The word "spirit" etymologically means breath. In human beings, this breath, or logos (meaning law become soul) draws together all we do, live, breathe, think, pray, manifest. We merely have to let go and allow the great power to come through our spiritual senses.

The soul around the Self is etched with our experiences from life to life, from age to age, as we go down that long path. Our experiences are recorded on the soul as we climb the ladder and go up the bootstrap path through the center of all being. We still do not know the soul in a concrete manner. We can only hope to know the soul a little better through experimental work, through working with the Self. We cannot demand to know it, for it is that part of us that has nothing to do with our objective material lives directly, with the exception of having control over the body systems. Objective knowledge is not enough. We must depend on the sensing of the soul and the soul essence subjectively. Although in working with the Self, if we have gone through God-Realization, we will notice that there are changes that take place in the perimeter around the soul.

We discover that the soul has a divine nature that is of God. If we recognize God as the great divine power and intelligence that animates the universe, we can readily see and understand how the soul is a part of that intelligence and power. God and the soul are divine because both represent the infinite and supreme, the everlasting, the ever moving, the record of all being, and the First Cause and principle of all creation to the mystic. This supreme, infinite Cause is divine. In no other sense do we mean this word and in no other sense is it applied. Therefore, we say that our soul is part of the Divinity.

Why is it there? How did it come to be there? What is its part in the scheme of creation? What purpose does the soul serve as a divine and immortal element residing temporarily within the human body? These questions should be diligently followed up.

If we look only materially at these questions, we see that the soul serves no purpose not already served by the physical functions of the material human being. That is the very foundation of why the soul is there. The soul is the infinite human being in memory, but not from a material point of view. The attempts to artificially produce life by spontaneous generation have proven unsuccessful even if the necessary elements were brought together. The life and vital forces that animate such generation were not present. Science seemed satisfied in the assumption that life was a purely chemical affair, molecules and elements acting upon one another.

Such a theory would eliminate the vital principles of Divinity from the explanation of who we are as human beings. Our brain would be all there was, just intellectual chemical reactions. Consciousness would then become action and reaction due to the material stimuli of minerals and elements. Life would come primarily from the air breathed into the lungs, bringing with it a certain vitalizing energy, just as an electrical current animates a motor with nothing divine, nothing superphysical, nothing pertaining to the soul. The soul would not have a place in the scheme of things. For science, the soul does not exist.

Even most theological explanations for the existence of the soul do not make the soul a necessary attribute. In these explanations nothing passes from life to life because they leave out the reincarnations. They leave out the experiences of those who know they have lived before. Continuous existence calls in the problem of the soul because something has to move from life to life. Something had to – just had to – know how this body worked so that its autonomic system would work readily, freely and in perfect rhythm. That rhythm, that perfection, came out of the divine essence within our soul – the divinity to make us simply an image of God and nothing more.

It also had an effect on our moral development. The pursuit of the soul falls short of meaning if the soul were placed in us simply to give us an immortal attribute – something to live after physical death and await a day of spiritual existence. This is not practical. The only purpose served by such an example of reason for the soul's existence would be to foster the theological idea of a final judgment – the day when all the souls released from the earth from millions of years would come together to be judged and suffer punishment or reward.

This idea has long since shown to be totally illogical. It is not in keeping with nature, its laws or principles. Therefore, it couldn't be of God.

There is another reason for the existence of the soul. Mystics and philosophers have said that when we are Self-conscious and aware of our existence, which the soul makes possible, then we realize ourselves because the Self is the Self of God – a part of it. It is a cell in the being and body of our great Creator. We shall contemplate the reality of God and see what our consciousness of God is when we exist in that consciousness and when we are in tune with God's being.

The terms individuality and personality are used interchangeably and should not be so. The dictionary makes the two almost synonymous. Personality cannot pertain solely to one's physical countenance, material body or appearance. One's personality may reveal itself, or even veil itself, in the clothes one wears, or in the manner of physical expression, e.g. one's home, furnishings, books, friends, hobbies and pleasures. Personality may be revealed or veiled. Personality is that subtle quality of the inner person that reveals itself in our traits and characteristics. Actually, our personality is the sum total of many lifetimes brought together in the soul, which is around the Self. It is the reflection and reaction of our many lifetimes and our much learning, much error and much development. It is not really something that has anything to do with the outer person, in a sense, except that it is reflected there.

The individuality, on the other hand, pertains solely to those materialistic qualities, attributes and expressions that constitute time-limited traits. The outer manifestation plus education, habits, thoughts and beliefs is the wearing of the physical body and the physical world. We are wearing a body. It is a vehicle that is carrying you, the Self and the soul.

The personality is the naked body under the unchangeable cloak of soul. It is you. We are wearing a body. The individuality is the cloak we have taken on and gives us our outward appearance.

The soul personality is most concerned with our earthly existence through our many reincarnations. Reincarnation is for the purpose of evolving the soul personality and attaining Self-mastery. The lessons we learn with our soul personality enable us to progress in the process of evolution. Because, whether we know it or not, the subtle forces of the soul are functioning as long as we are in this material body. Our soul personality expresses in each incarnation. We bring with us the knowledge of the physical functions. In simple words, in reality, the personality is the mind of the soul. It carries that record of wisdom and knowledge.

Individuality can be said to be the brain of the material body. We distinguish between mind and brain. The brain is the organ through which the thoughts of the mind are experienced. The subjective faculties of the mind are referred to as the mind of the soul. Personality is the soul storehouse of memories. If we assume that in a single incarnation the lessons learned today are preserved for us tomorrow, a year or ten years from now, we must admit that the memory has its faults as a storehouse of facts, experiences, pictures and impressions. The conscious mind can distort and forget memories, but the soul registers the essence of our experience.

The materialist may claim that the memory and its storehouse are functions of the brain – a physical thing associated with a subtle mind of an unknown soul. We must point out that the brain can prevent the brain from remembering a past impression. An injury to the brain will affect recollection and conscious memory. A blow to the head may remove the desire to eat or drink. But not even the materialist would claim that this proves the injury removes or destroys the existence of hunger or thirst in the body. The brain is an organ of the body through which the emotions and desires are consciously realized and find their power to function. Injury to the brain affects the conscious objectification of facts and impressions. The brain is very much like a prism.

We may obstruct or close the passage that leads from the inner subjective to the outer objective chamber. But shutting off the passage does not destroy the thought. Also, the blockage does not prove the non-existence of the chamber beyond. Having no recall of memories in the injured brain is not proof that the memory resides in the material outer chamber of the brain. Paralysis may mute the expression of every human faculty and muscle to the extent of there being no sign of intelligence. But the mind will continue to think and have many thoughts within that are unable to be expressed objectively.

The reality is that the mind we use is part of the mind of God. If we admit the possibility of the existence of a storehouse of memory, in which all facts and impressions consciously realized are stored for future use, it is just a little point to yield that this Great Architect of the structure of the human body can store experiences in memory forever. The soul remembers the temple of experience and stores everything there. This is the chamber of pleasures and sorrows, the school of lessons learned, the chart of likes and dislikes, the encyclopedia of facts, the court of justice and retention, the record of impression, the resort of test and trial, the tribunal of decision between the rights and wrongs. These combinations constitute, in each existence, the personality of the human being. Human Being. This is our being, being alive in this particular existence.

But we could be alive in another existence, in another world entirely, and still use the same function – the same mind. We might even be another type of body, but the mind would be the same.

The ancient Egyptians were the forerunners of all modern secret societies and mystery schools. Many of their symbolic ceremonies and rites have been passed down to this day. There is much evidence, not only of belief in the soul, but of considerable understanding of its origin, nature and purpose. They said duality because we had two bodies, but really we have four. The Egyptians recognized the inner, divine nature, or our soul, known to them as RA. RA was the sun and the life force coming in, symbolized in the form of a bird. This symbol represented the flight into eternity of the soul after death – namely, after the transition of the body. Soul was symbolized by the lotus flower, the unfolding, everlasting, the white, the being, the perfect, the unblemished that flourished in the rich soil along the Nile. The mystical concepts of the ancient Egyptians were highly evolved.

In the Orphic religious practices of the 6th century B.C., the soul was considered a divine element, which was evolving through earthly expression. The soul was a part of the divine and universal. The body in its limited and mortal condition was but the womb or prison. The continuous existence of the soul and the body together was a punishment for sins in a previous condition. They believed in the homogeneity of all living things and the transmigration of the soul. It was taught that the soul was entombed in the animal, earthly body for that length of time that would enable it to gradually attain perfection during its contact with matter (John Milton's Secret Laws of the Orphic Rites).

When the soul has attained perfection, it is freed from the cycle of generation and no longer requires contact with these conditions, tests, trials and re-cycling. It again becomes a pure and evolved soul that returns to its divine source as before its imprisonment.

Most mystics believed that the soul is a divine essence, different from the physical body. Philosophers born about 301 B.C. held that the sun was the abode of God. From the sun radiated a divine essence, the soul of God. This soul pervades all space and, in separable segments, enters into the human body to be born on earth. The soul essence is the revivification of the fire or the universal emanation of the intelligence provided by God. The vitality of the soul after death depends on the degree of its vitality during its life in the body. The soul is a divine element, having its origin in God. It resides temporarily in the body and is freed at the dissolution of the body to return to its origin.

To really understand what life is, we must begin to see and know that all of this and the great wonders that we see around us must have something that remembers from life to life, that which we are and that which we are going to be. We are not going to be just a person; we are going to be beings. We are going to be highly intelligent. If we listen to the words of the inner being and reach a state of spiritual consciousness, we will soon realize that there has to be a soul, for many of the answers and things we get would be impossible without a record brought forward from other incarnations. It is not possible, after considerable thought, to conceive of our having a soul without conceiving of our expression on earth as body and soul. The material form encloses the immaterial that has continual existence.

Consider the soul as a separate part and shell of the Self – the immortal parts of the dual human being. Mind must naturally be considered the immaterial entity of the being, immortal, divine and imminently from God. This is the reality. This is the actual heritage that God has left us that we can take with us: our life history, our life library from one life to another.

SOUL III

Down through the years and in the course of our striving to attain initiation, Illumination by the light of Christ, we have heard many instructions about letting go and letting God. We may have heard about the need to kill the ego and other parts of ourselves. This killing the ego would actually be a very sad thing to do because we would not be worth very much to Jesus Christ or the glorious Creator, the Nameless One, without all our parts.

The earth and the intelligence of its substance has helped and aided us in producing this physical body. It is sometimes a body of clay because of the way we have used it, and we have allowed it to hamper and master us rather than we mastering it. This body is the temple in which we, soul and Self, reside. It is in this soul and Self that dwells the record of our many lifetimes, and our attainment which is the attunement with the pure consciousness of God and the Masters Jesus and Mary.

It is the temple where we take on the Illumination of the light of Christ and that light so infuses into the physical substance of the body that the body is transmuted. The degree to which it is transmuted is determined by the amount of light we receive and the degree to which we permit it to take over our body. In other words, it depends on the degree to which we get ourselves out of the way.

That which is real and within this physical body is an inseparable part of the infinite soul. It is in attunement with the mind of God and part of the great oversoul, bridging all space and time. Our soul is the sheath of the Self and is a cell in the body of our Lord Jesus Christ, and therefore, it is a part of the body of God, God's mind, or Akasha. Because if we are part of the Body of Christ, we cannot help but be a part of our Nameless Creator.

In the words of the old masters: To the degree that we attain Self-mastery, we will to that degree change from the normal density of the masses of people's bodies, to the transmuted physical body, where that body is partially light. This light is strong enough to be seen. We can see it with our physical eyes.

In the New Testament, when Jesus had prepared himself after the resurrection, He ascended. And it was in a completely transmuted body, because the physical had been rebuilt when He returned and rose after the crucifixion.

The soul will express itself differently in my body than it would in another through habit, education, temperament and the effect of many lifetimes of learning. I may through habit and education prevent the soul from demonstrating to the same degree of purity of understanding of God's creation and God's Word. Two souls might receive the same words, the same facts, the same educational materials, but due to their different experiences, may not pick those up and receive them in the same way. This is due to their personalities. It does not have anything to do directly with their individualities, which are a passing, material thing that can change anytime. Individuality is something that we can leave behind when we pass through transition to the other worlds.

That which is a part of God is infinite and is not separate, but is a unified part. It is not independent but dependent. Here is the foundation and basis of the term unity and fellowship, sisterhood, brotherhood with God and people. The individuality is the force that we set in action and determine, and is totally of our own creation. This is called by many of the churches "sins of the flesh."

Both personality and character are ever in the making. Our personality slowly evolves by spiritual reflection and the light of the soul. What is recorded in the soul slowly evolves within us and this evolution manifests itself not only in the spiritual sphere to which the soul belongs, but right here on the earth plane while the soul is within the body. If the eternal light in us is unhampered and pure, it radiates the light of God, God's first-born Son, the Lord of the Sun. This is the light of Christ in us.

All colors are vibrations of the same white light but appear different in the personality when filtered through an earthly medium. So too, the soul retains a distinct personality, which it never loses. The essence of the soul is always part of the cosmic soul, which manifests in millions of expressions, and resides at the core of every personality. Each of these expressions represents another person, another personality. The complete Cosmic Soul cannot be lost because the essence of these personalities blends into it, just as the many colors of the spectrum cannot be lost when they are again assembled and passed through a prism, blending into pure white light.

When we study the mysteries, we can get so complicated that we lose the simplicity of God's great creation and start to separate one art from another, like astrology. We separate it from the New Testament and philosophy. This is a fallacy because there is only one God and one creation. Expressions like astrology have to be part and parcel of the same truth, totally united with all other facets of truth. So let us now look at the ten planets of this solar system to which we attribute certain functions or personalities. For instance, the planet Mars is said to have an effect on the red blood cells. We say it has an effect on disposition or temper, influencing the volatile disposition of a person. It is a force in action.

When we say that Venus is the planet of love, we have a perfect example of personality and individuality. Venus, when it is harmoniously aspected, meaning it has a good relationship to our sun sign or some other planets, brings an adorable nature. It has a tendency to give us at birth a great deal of love for others. It increases the potential of physical love. But when it is inharmoniously aspected with another heavenly body, we would find our love influence was not as pure and as Selfless as it was when it was well aspected. The planet Venus is the planet of love. That is its personality. But the way we use it or the way it is aspected relative to other heavenly bodies, what its electromagnetic influence is on that other planet in our birth chart, this denotes our individuality. It is the individuality of the planet Venus at the time of our birth.

Therefore, souls on the cosmic plane never leave it except to reincarnate here in an earthly body, but they can and do project their personalities onto other personalities on the earth plane. They do this in an effort to help those whom they are able to reach here. Those who are highly enough evolved or attuned to receive the help constructively can experience this.

The personality is to the soul as the psychic body is to the physical body. For the psychic body is the effluent material that fills the spiritual body and gives effervescence through the physical.

The soul does not lose its personality through the change called death or transition. Neither does our personality change when we extend ourselves in communication with others on the earth plane. The dictionary defines personality as the habitual patterns and qualities of behavior of a person as expressed by physical and mental activity and attitudes. It is the quality of being a person, not an animal, not a demon, not a stone, but that which constitutes a person. It is a very interesting fact that in Latin the meaning is given as "mask," so we might say that the personality of the soul was its mask.

The individuality distinguishes one person from another. Personality is the naked body under the changeable cloak of individuality, which sort of reverses the Latin origin, since the word "individuality" comes from the meaning not to divide and indivisible. But when we look at this carefully, we will see that the individuality is not divisible because it will not move from this plane to another world and still be intact.

Our personality goes with us the same as the Self and soul. This is why Jesus said, **"If you save your life you shall lose it, but you who lose your life shall save it."** For when we let go of what we see in the mirror of our memory, or what we think we are and our actions, which is the individuality, then only may the pure being through our personality show forth. Our personality will then be reborn.

Within the personality is the storehouse of memory. Our personality is the combination of the impressions that we have acquired through many lifetimes along with the purity that we have been able to accept the great mind and that of our Lord Jesus Christ. This constitutes the existence of our personality, that of a human being existing within the mind and body of Christ.

Here we have a picture of cosmic forces in action: Personality forces blending together, creating the atmosphere of our personal universe. If it's sunny and shining, or rainy and cold, depends on our approach and our acceptance of what Jesus said: "I am the Way." For if we are traveling this way, we will have our personality that will be the totally overshadowing mask of our life.

We are not the outer physical form, color or size. Our appearance helps us in identifying ourselves to others on the physical level. We will no longer bother to judge, and we won't worry about whether we are heard or need to listen to the comments of others. For we have a greater realization, and this realization is that our soul is different from every other individual's soul. Therefore, no comparison is possible.

This is because everything we see and experience is filtered through the soul, so it is colored differently for each of us. The Self in each of us is exactly the same because that is the God part of us.

If we become dominated by any one major emotion or sentiment, the personality will reflect this, especially if it is untrue. The finer and more delicate our thoughts, the more attractive and harmonious our personality will be. The more we devote time to thinking that which arouses the gentler emotions, the more we will experience a most beautiful transformation of our personality and will be able to take on the mask of the Lord Jesus and Mary in a brief time.

FLESH BODY I

We are living in an age with a vastly different energy level than 100 years ago. We walk down streets with masses of wires around us, breathe air full of atomic energy, drink water full of fluorides and chlorine, eat food with phosphorus and other poisons, and work at a high pitch all the time. We are under a great deal of stress.

The normal tension level of nature has, by evolution, changed the cell functions in the last 150-200 years. We are reaching a new cell cycle, and it is necessary to break down the tension level. Sometimes we have to fast or take away meat for a few days. We each react differently to different foods, and we need to watch our chemical balance, maybe setting some foods aside temporarily. Until we can accept ourselves as perfect beings, we cannot keep our own bodies in balance.

We need to notice changes in the time of new moons and full moons. We don't need to set up charts as astrologers, but it is a good idea to have some idea of the stellar influences we are experiencing. We need to get some control of the forces around us. Our thinking in the past has been unconscious and unguarded. Now we need to think and comprehend in order to adapt to the changes taking place.

Leviticus 17:11 **"For the life of the flesh is in the blood; and I have given it for you upon the altar to make atonement for your souls; for it is the blood that makes atonement, by reason of the life."** The flesh body is the lowest descent of God's manifestation in the living bodies of earth. But the flesh is still the temple of God. I Corinthians 3:16-17 **"Do you not know that you are God's temple, and that God's Spirit dwells in you? If anyone destroys God's temple, God will destroy them. For God's temple is Holy, and that temple you are."**

The blood carries the record of life to the three seed atoms of life. The body and its desires are not evil. In this New Age we will show how to reconstruct the flesh body, by applying the truth teachings to our consciousness. We will attune our bodies to a higher rate of vibration. The flesh body is just raw matter, and needs to be clothed with the immortality of pure thought. Then the flesh is renewed and transmuted from mortality to immortality by the renewing of our mind.

Romans 12:1-3 Paul says, **"I appeal to you therefore brethren, by the mercies of God, to present your bodies as a living sacrifice, holy and acceptable to God, which is your spiritual worship." "For by Grace given to me, I bid every one of you not to think of yourself more highly than you ought to think."**

The Laws of the Flesh Body are 1. Right body function; 2. Right breathing; 3. Right thinking; 4. Right action; 5. Right prideless humility; 6. Right Mindfulness; 7. Tolerance in Love.

The discipline of the body must be as strict as the student needs to be stimulated into spiritual action. The disciplines must be vigorously and diligently observed in order to reconstruct and control the Kundalini force so that the body may enter into the realization itself, the Self.

In Romans Chapter 8 we find the transformation of the physical body through the Spirit of Christ and the redemption of the flesh through the spiritual nature of the divine Christ. It is emphasized again that there is no condemnation in Christ Jesus but that the nature of our carnal bodies is in constant variance with the Laws of God. We call it carnal mind, showing that the erroneous concept of sin rules the flesh body. This is a misconception of the universal mind caused by mass mind and the finite portion of the non-illumined brain. The flesh body will transgress the Law, or sin, because in this stage it is carnal.

Matthew 5:29-30 **"And if your right eye offend you, cut it off, and cast it from you: For it is profitable for you that one of your members should perish, and not that your whole body should be cast into hell. And if your right hand offend you, cut it off, and cast if from you: for it is profitable for you that one of your members should perish, and not your whole body should be cast into hell."**

Often our mental concepts about the creation of the flesh body become spiritualized or sanctified and separate from mass mind through the Illumination of the Christ Light. The flesh body is the vehicle through which the Creator manifests and is continually creating within. It is in the flesh body that power is made ever present. That power is generated in the spiritual body that then transfers the God energy into the physical as power for the sons and daughters of God. Every organ of the body has both a physical and a spiritual function.

Jesus said in Matthew 22:26, **"And as they were eating, Jesus took bread, and blessed it, and broke it, and gave it to the disciples, and said, 'Take, eat; this is my Body.'"**

God took the body out of which we were formed from those things that God created from nothingness into something. That mass was the extract of all creatures, elements, all stars in heaven and earth, all properties, essences, and natures. God extracted the most subtle and most excellent in all these and united them into one mass. From this we were created. So we are a microcosm or a little world, because we are formed from the whole firmament. We are the quintessence taken from the stars, planets, and the four elements of the earth. So we are the fifth, that is fifth or quintessence, beyond the four elements.

Between the microcosm and macrocosm, there is a difference of form, image, species, and substance. Our earth is our flesh; our water is the blood; our heat is the fire; our sinew is the air. Only the substance of our body has changed the appearance of these basic elements. So we are human beings, not a world, yet made from the world, made in the likeness of God. Yet we comprise in ourselves all the qualities of the world.

The scriptures rightly say we are dust and ashes, and into ashes we will return. We are the image of God, not like the world, having flesh and blood, but still more than the world. We are dust and ashes. We should keep this in mind so we are not led astray. We should ponder what we have been, what we are now, and what we will be hereafter.

Matter is not limited to the inorganic, since it manifests as the organic as well. What differentiates the two? Inorganic matter is lifeless; that is, it cannot assimilate, grow, and reproduce itself. Organic matter is the same whether simple or complex, but is infused with the life force. It can assimilate, grow and reproduce itself, like animals, vegetables and human beings. Inorganic matter is increased by external action entirely, while organic matter assimilates matter within itself and grows or evolves from a single cell to the complex organism of the human body.

MATTER CANNOT MAKE MATTER AND LIFE CANNOT MAKE LIFE, FOR MATTER EXISTS AND LIFE EXISTS. Life uses matter in making the proper vehicles for itself, but it never uses crystals in the building of the body if it can avoid them. Organic matter follows a definite law following the center and circumference of a circle. Thus matter manifests according to the triangle, and life according to the idea of the circle.

Let us remember that the spiritual body functioned the same way 20,000 years ago, 10,000 years ago, and 5,000 years ago. When we think of it in this way, we wonder if we adore our Creator enough.

Our bodies changed over time in accord with our use of feet, hands and limbs. We are water animals, conceived and born in water. We have an affinity for water and air, a water creature adapting to air. We should remember this in connection with healing. We are renewing every cell, as well as our whole skin, hour by hour (50,000,000 explosions inside the human body). People evolving in the tropics developed dark skin. Those in the woods grew taller and stronger. Those living on vegetables grew differently than those who ate meat. Our admiration for mountainous country is a subconscious remembrance of the necessity to seek protection and hunt in them.

Water is the main essential element in our health. We throw off water and perspiration through skin, urine and breath. Elimination of materials through the kidneys, bladder and bowels are the three phases of elimination. Exercise is needed for balance. It relaxes the physical and lets the spiritual express itself, regulating the glandular functions. Proper breathing affects the flow of spirit, the ethereal connection between spiritual and physical, and affects the electrical structure or spiritual body.

FLESH BODY II

The human body is constantly wearing out and being renewed, revitalized and regenerated. None of us today are the same in our bodies as we were a few years or even a few months ago. The ancients used to say that when a child was born, death begins in the body. Science confirms this teaching and shows that combustion, destruction, depreciation and breakdown, wear and tear on all parts of the body. This process of breaking down is so completely destructive in nature that an 80th of the entire weight of the physical body is destroyed every twenty-four hours.

Of course, a person who lives a more sedentary life does not destroy their body as rapidly as a hard working person. One 80th is about average for most of us. At this rate, our body would be destroyed or consumed in about eighty days. We cannot live eighty days without food or water because we would pass away from weakness as more than half our cells would have wasted away. Careful tests show that without food, death will occur when about half of the body has been consumed or depleted. This would take the average person about forty days.

The exception to this would be a person who had a certain discipline and spiritual direction and had attained a definite spiritual reality. They would have to be able to receive energy and strength from the magnetic forces of the earth and from our Creator. They would not have to eat and drink as much as the uninitiated.

Starving to lose weight is an improper method because we need certain foods to be able to go long periods. There is an art to fasting as there is with every other form of healing. Starving causes the body to consume its own substance, which may be dangerous. We have to reduce body weight by drawing upon the fuel stored in the fat between the tissues. If we consume the fat cells, then the weight comes off. Gradually, the body consumes an 80th of that weight every twenty-four hours and throws off water in proportion to the cellular breakdown through the kidneys and bladder. If we want to reduce our weight, we should do this under supervision of one who knows the art of fasting. We need someone who can write us a good dietary plan and who knows the chemistry of what is going on with nutrition. We need to maintain our vitality as we slough off the majority of wastes and weight in the water eliminated.

During absorption in the digestion process, some fat molecules are not broken down and dissolved but are carried through the body to certain fat pockets in the body where the fat is stored for future use. If we take in more than we need, fat cells are distributed between layers of tissues and in places where there are not ordinarily fat pockets. These fat cells add unnecessary weight. Some fat cells are sent to important sites, like the pericardial sac around the heart, so the heart can pump inside a bag of lubricant, so it has ease and protection of movement.

As we eat and drink to sustain life, we need the proper food and proper breathing in order to consume the old materials. The blood is constantly being cleansed and is forming new cells. We can easily see how the skin peels off in small scales and is always renewing itself. The hair is constantly renewing itself, as well as teeth and bones. So we become what we eat.

Eating the wrong food tends to destroy more rapidly the healthy parts of the body. There are just as many good foods as undesirable ones. Part of the cause of disease can be found in the diet. Even with good foods, certain combinations are not good for our particular metabolism. A standard rule of thumb is to ingest vegetables at a different time than we ingest fruits, because the fruits digest much more rapidly and use entirely different enzymes to break them down than vegetables.

Chemists know that mixing two chemicals can have a destructive result, while using them alone is safe and helpful. Sometimes it is not the mixing but the processing of the food that is the problem. Certain foods, when cooked, are better separated from other foods because when combined they produce a chemical war in the stomach or digestive system. This produces gas, fermentation and poisons that injure the blood and destroy tissue. Other foods may have good minerals and proteins in them, but too much of them will cause trouble. We can absorb only moderate amounts, but when we increase the quantity, the destructive effects will proliferate through the body.

For instance, drinking coffee or caffeinated tea in large quantities is not good for the body. Black coffee is more harmful when combined with cream or sugar. Milk added causes undesirable poisons and disturbance. The more exotic and fancy the restaurant or kitchen, the more likely the combinations will cause some trouble.

Never eat all you can hold, always leave the table just a little hungry. This will keep you away from digestive problems. Drink juices and liquids away from your solid food, except when drinking wine. Liquids digest easily and quickly and interfere with the digestion of solid matter. Sip during the meal, but do not drink a lot when eating.

The intestines are divided into two sections, small and large. The small intestine is approximately twenty feet in length and can expand to a diameter of three inches. Food rubs against the villi that are small hair cell projections. During this twenty feet of movement through the intestines, the mysterious work of absorbing vitamins, minerals, proteins, fats and carbohydrates is done. Vitality, strength and necessary

113

chemical elements are pulled from the food. The villi projections act like little suckers pulling enzymes and nutrients through the cells into the bloodstream. They absorb what they want and transmit it to the proper parts of the body. The food is stationary for a few minutes to absorb the materials and then the tube automatically contracts, squeezed by the nerves, pushing the food on through the canal.

The body is able to maintain perfect equilibrium and heat inside. It is not just the blood and its temperature that warms the body. The subconscious mind takes care of the heating process, fighting a very difficult battle in the process. No matter how cold it gets outside, the body has to maintain the same temperature inside. We may feel cold in the morning or in the rain or snow, but our experience of cold is outside on the skin. It is not due to any change of temperature on the inside of our bodies. In fact, we can walk out of a sauna where we have been sweating and suffering from the heat and plunge right into icy water without changing the temperature on the inside of our bodies. The person living at the equator where the temperature is 120 degrees during the day has the same internal temperature as the Eskimo living at the North Pole where there are constant sub-zero temperatures.

Metabolism and combustion in the body control much of the temperature regulation. Certain carbohydrates, especially sugars, cause fermentation in the intestines, and this forms alcohol and fumes that are combusted by a chemical process and turned into heat. One pint of alcohol is created in the body every twenty-four hours for the purpose of heating the body. This pint is mostly fumes but has some liquid content to it. It is used almost as soon as it is created, so there are never more than a few ounces in the body at any given time.

Cooling is just as important in the body as heating. The subconscious mind looks after the heat on the inside so that it never gets too hot except in disease when some toxins need

114

sloughing off. Destroying tissues and fighting germs then requires heat. The skin is the largest organ of the body and contains small pores through which the subconscious mind causes an oily liquid to form, cooling the outer flesh. It is not the oily liquid that cools, but the evaporation of the perspiration that keeps airing and cooling the surface of the skin so that it does not scorch too rapidly. Perspiring freely is a sign of health, while not being able to perspire shows that something is wrong with the cuticle of the skin that is preventing the pores from functioning properly. Air must go back in through the pores where the moisture comes out, and this gives the entire body a breathing method, in addition to the air we breathe into our lungs. Dirt filling these pores will eventually cause disease. Painting a person with paint or metallic liquids causes abnormal conditions in a person in a short time.

Our thinking and will power influence our healthy functioning. We have seen demonstrations of a person concentrating on their arm in a fairly cold room. The arm will begin to perspire quite freely and to exude more moisture than it had before, while the rest of the body remained cold and without any perspiration. This simple example proves that our minds control the important things in our lives.

WORD I

The Word is ever-present, ever misunderstood, ever in action and in rest, and gives, when understood, life to the dead and strength to the weak. Pronounce it not, for it is worthless to anyone who does not know its correct pronunciation, or when and how it should be used. It is worthless to anyone who knows it not as the finest ruby so overlaid with encrustations that its light cannot be seen.

In Egypt that word was known and others joined hands with its actions as they invested the earth with its sound and its perfume. Stand in awe in its presence. We humble our hearts when we see it. Gaze upon its ineffableness and ask that the Highest may assist you. Held within the hidden universe is all this, and the peace that comes through the enlightenment is the great. Slowly unfolds the rose – in color seen – the perfume sensed, and the properties held within each when seen, known and understood, the soul becomes its origin.

Silence then becomes known – the red ruby shines in its might – the right encircles the inspiring, and the love comprehends. As dawn in its radiance, the color the ruby sheds its roseate over the falling and rising of all things. Have you, o reader, comprehended? All writing is far from plain, for language conceals more than it reveals. The heartthrob is unknown to all but the one – a smile may linger on the lips and the pain be concealed from any and all except the one!

The tragedies of life are but moments along the mighty way – each and all serving as lessons, and they who make their mark when passing down the mountain will see them on their return. Then has our accomplishment begun, for recognition is first when in the ascendant.

Before we pass on from this, we do so with all kindness for those who see not, nor know. The voice of God may be so great as to deafen some and awaken others. Then it becomes necessary to use other means than the voice, although they are the same but appear different.

When considering anything we receive that is repugnant, the first consideration to settle in mind is the accuracy of the statement made. It is impossible in some cases to demonstrate the accuracy to anyone who presupposes that they are receptive to some extent; and what to one is folly is logic to another. In such a condition as has been set forth, proof is only possible when the mind and all its faculties are receptive to truth, and that means that all preconceptions are placed at least in abeyance.

We now enter into another point that briefly is this: the passions of mind are not always demonstrable to the student. Mind attempting to fathom mind is often an impossibility. It can only be conceived through control. To conceive of anything, there must be a lower and a higher. The lower cannot be expected to receive the higher in its completeness, but the higher can and does conceive of the lower in its many parts. Any lesson of any height will necessarily be hard to grasp by the brain, for the brain is a falling force and not an ascending one. Mind, the attribute of the soul, debased by the Fall, cannot completely conceive of soul, its parent. It has become so enmeshed in this lower world that to see and to conceive, it must be penetrated by the higher.

As we look at mind, there comes into view its progenitor, Self, that part which has been sent out from the house of its Origin and has become a wanderer. Wandering to find its plane of action it has taken refuge in humankind, using the brain and the physical organs of expression.

Between our minds and that of others, there is of necessity a link, strong in some, weak in others. Let us consider the human mind. Mind says to the brain, "I have taken refuge in you, o physical organ of expression, for to me you are capable of much. And as I tarry along the way, you are now my instrument of expression. But at some time I will leave you and go into another which will suit me the better, for I cannot remain with you longer." The physical organ responds, "I accept you as your home for a time, for I, too, am not to be without a tenant. For the blankness of non-occupancy is very hard on me. As for you, you must make of me what you can, for I am very finite."

The two are not at all times in harmony, for the brain often fails to register and transmit what the mind wishes. Then there is a conflict that disorders both the physical and the mind and the many organs having relation to them. Then you have so-called insanity, which is but discordant impulses, due to faulty registering and transmission. Between them there is induced a condition strongly affecting the organs. This faulty registering is sometimes due to a poorly evolved brain or a poorly receiving brain in its peripheral parts. Add to this the confusion in the higher ethereal parts that cause the many impulses to faultily impact upon the brain. These are not all the elements to be taken into consideration in such cases.

Within mind there is a small element in ascent – this affects us but little until we are well enough evolved to receive, and such are few. Nevertheless, we proceed to demonstrate how we struggle against adversity and pass upward in spite of such drawbacks. The many inequalities lead to traits of character, some good, some bad, all of which play a part. The differences may cause actions that others judge a crime and many other actions by whatever name. When the philanthropic and aggressive instincts meet, there is genius. When the level is affected and on a high plane we have one no longer reincarnating. These are ones who become masters, for their plane is so high that they function evenly – the balance is maintained. Such a one passes to the higher realms and becomes emancipated from earth's thrall. They are rapidly elevated for they have overcome the inertia and are passing swiftly into such heights as are beyond the ken of mind.

Mind has then ceased to be the great functioning part and occupies a subordinate position. It is required to do only the most ordinary acts to meet the requirements of life on earth. The act of receiving and then following the inner guidance is all that is necessary to do. We deal not so much with the brain as we do with factors influencing it.

We are part of the many kinds and they of us. Those who can reach and know this consciously and not by rote repetition of words, have become part of the university of nature. Having mastered, we become masters. We are then conscious of the whole and do not need to remain on the earth except as a sacrifice to do the acts of greatness – or smallness – in service. These ones are seldom widely known and are often little appreciated by those of earth, whose standards are different.

In the beginning was God. We are not interested in where God began. We are interested in God, for it was the Word God gave that is the creative Cause, first started in function. And this is the beginning of any created thing, either of God, the Hierarchy, or human beings. Perhaps we could say that in the beginning we have the springtime of the planting of the seed of Causation, before any objective thing is created.

This reality, to which we have given the name 'God,' is an ever-present fact in our experience. The Word as spoken by the Creator, the infinite and universal creative Spirit, is the activator of symbolism. In reality, the Creator contains imagination, knowingness and intelligence expressing through means of the Law. This Law is the format that is the Self-exacting intelligence of the Creator in action. Within this intelligence, the potentiality of the function of all things exists.

God is absolute intelligence, limitless imagination, with the all-encompassing consciousness of complete Self-expression.

The Spirit makes things out of itself, through inner acting upon itself, the act of God acting on consciousness. In other words, it is the inner consciousness of the Creator acting upon itself that releases the power into a given form. Within the nature of this Spirit, its own nature, there is a Law obeying the will of God.

Self-contemplation is an awareness of the core of Self. It is being conscious of its duality as absolute everything and absolute nothing. The Word of God transmitted through us brings an inner sense of being that must be completed. For this is the original Cause working through the sound of our mind and voice. Therefore God must be forever expressing and must always be perfect and harmonious. The answers which come from the Self will be perfect, reflecting the original creative Cause. Were the answers to be anything but perfect, they would be Self-destructive.

All words are symbols. When we use a word, The First Cause becomes evident in the absolute intelligence of God, and the Spirit motivates the action through the body, conveying the meaning in back of the words. The creative intelligence continues to create because this intelligence never completely came into being.

Jesus simplified this in his words, **"For the words that I speak to you, I speak not of myself, but the Father who dwells in Me, He does the works."**

For this is the mind of God working in us and through us. For God can work for us only by working through us.

The creative power of God manifests itself through imagination, will and feeling. As the creative mind of the universe operates upon itself through its will, imagination and feeling, it creates forms which are subject to it and its Law, but which have no reality apart from the mind which creates them. It is the creative mind that Jesus used, and that we may all use for conscious purposes to attain Self-knowingness.

WORD II

The Word, as spoken of in Genesis and in the first chapter of John, refers to the spoken Word of God. The Word can either be written or spoken with equal effect. Consider the following facts:

1. The written word is symbolic and if properly written, conveys a message that is recreated in our minds, and thereby effective.

2. The spoken word is a symbol of power, and has both the basic energy and the creative power of God in it. **"In the beginning was the Word, and the Word was with God...and the Word became flesh."**

Human beings are the manifestation of the active Word of God. God said it and it was done. We say it, and it is and shall be done. Jesus was known as the Logos or Word. We are the many-membered sons/daughters of the Creator. We are the extensions of God's spoken Word. When we reach the state where we speak from the Self, then we become the Word of God in flesh.

The written word is merely the symbolic combination of the power of the spoken word to the person reading them. God said, **"Let there be light,"** and there was light. Here we have the potential and the Spirit. God activated the power in the voice, and the Word of God was manifested. Everything was created in the beginning by the great Word through the projection into space of divine creative power.

The Creator is God in the act of creating, and is the Supreme Being, Nameless, but with supreme will, a will-power which the Egyptians called "RA." The word, or "rite" is from Sanskrit "riti," meaning "a going-away," from the Aryan, "ri" meaning "to flow." In this sense, using a writ is using the word, since

123

rites or writs help us to understand the way, by causing a flow to the form that depicts the desired result. Jesus said in Matthew 4:4, **"Man shall not live by bread alone, but by every word that proceeds from the mouth of God."**

We can evaluate the statement of Jesus: **"Think not what goes into the mouth, but what comes out of the mouth that defiles the soul."** Jesus spoke many things and they took place instantly. In the Upper Room He said, **"All these things I do, so shall you do also, and even greater than these."** In Matthew 8:16, **"That evening they brought to Him many possessed with demons, and He cast out the spirits with a word."**

This will help us to understand the reality of the word, **"In the beginning was the Word, and the Word was with God."** So likewise is the Word with us, if we are conscious of the Master. If we are conscious of God, it is with us. The term "word" is used more than 575 times in the New Testament.

The Word comes by vibration with form. As we have a desire, so do we give it form, producing sound over which the light travels. In the art of healing, if one is being healed and hears the Word, it apparently works better for the less enlightened. If there is within us a part that can accept the words, this aids the healing. The Word is projection of sound into the physical realm of manifestation by the power of sound. Sound must have form, and a force. In back of all of this is the motivation of mind.

When we speak the Word, we respond to forms, sound of letters, and the package that is sent out. The motivation of mind is one thing; if we merely repeat it, the word drops to the floor. But if we give it life with feeling, we send it out because we want it to take form, and manifest. It is sometimes said that because of the vowel sounds that the Word gains life through the intelligence of mind. It manifests at that moment because there is but one mind and one consciousness.

The Word of God was spoken once, and God has held it ever since in silent, everlasting prayer. It had all the increments of sound, frequency, wavelength, power, force and motivation of mind. It became flesh, because it carried all of the wavelengths consistent with the chemical elements. The tongue, the two-edged sword, with its vibration and the sounding box of the roof of the mouth, produces radiation or sound waves. When we speak words, actual energy comes out and emits vibrations that are neither positive nor negative into the atmosphere.

Power travels along the sound track of the voice, and no other way. For the Word of God was soundless, because it was within God, in another dimension within which we live. Thus it is that the Word of God was left with us, for it echoes eternally within the being of the Creator. The Spirit of God gives it life, for this was God's feeling. The movement within God brings breath. The great Self develops the form.

There are two ways of speaking: you can speak through the lips, or through the solar plexus, where one's words take on dimension. This occurs because the solar plexus is taking the life force from the Self, for it is from the Self that we can gain God-consciousness. The ability to make sound is taken from the breath. The palate and the muscle tissues of the throat vibrate because of the breath. The breath passes through two channels, producing sounds that are both positive and negative. All spoken sounds are nearly-rounded tops to the waves. The breath with its life force forms a carrier that the voice travels over.

Words without feeling are flat and not creative. Words with the adrenaline of anger have feeling that vibrates. They create temporarily and this creative word has impact, but it returns to you, because it is not male. It is all feeling. The true creative word must have balance, both masculine and feminine.

The auditory stimulation picks up frequencies between 20 and 20,000 cycles per second. Below twenty we could not hear it, and it would not be sound. Six cycles per second with volume is lethal. Normal hearing has a range of 30 to 13,000 cycles per second. Water is the best conductor of sound. The speed of sound is about 741 miles per hour.

Sound in the Spirit is entirely reversed, as everything is reversed on the spiritual plane, polarity and directionally, from what is on the material plane. The state in which the illumined person works is as neutral as nature.

The ability to make sound is taken from the breath, or comes from the voice of the spirit in deep contemplation. Sound coming from the mouth is also controlled by the adrenals and mind. The negative forms, like cries and shock responses, are controlled by the adrenal glands. When we speak, we use the same energy as when we create a child. Remember, the gas through which the Kundalini force of the spine moves, the stuff spoken of in the 23rd Psalm, which is the creative energy used by the brain and sex forces, are the same forces used in speech.

The Word is only valid if it flows from the original divine source and is in harmony with God's will. God is not going to work through words of revenge or hate, except that they rebound in time on the speaker. God will work in harmony with the Laws of the universe and there is no limit to God's creative power. The only limit is in the degree of our ability to become pure, clear channels for their operation. It is best to choose our own words to fit a situation, brief powerful words that are easy to remember, held constantly before us until the matter is brought to pass. Let's not strain over them, beyond doing what we reasonably can in a physical way to bring things about. Let's leave the matter in God's hands. It may take a little time, but if the need is valid and our faith is sure, invisible doors will open to our good and invisible hands will lead us.

Let the word of our mouth speak of our coming life. Words bring down to earth. Meditation lifts up. Think and speak only that which is true, kind, helpful and necessary. Remember, the tongue was once an unruly member. God said, **"If you utter what is precious and not what is useless, you shall be as my mouth."**

Hebrews 4:12, **"For the Word of God is alive and active. It cuts more keenly than any two-edged sword, piercing as far as the place where life and spirit, joints and marrow divide. It sifts the purpose and thoughts of the heart."**

MIND I

All through the teaching of Jesus in the New Testament and the ancient mystery teachings runs the great golden thread of the mental law. Our ability to demonstrate the supremacy of spiritual thought force over all apparent material resistance must necessarily depend on our understanding of mental laws. We use the term "mental law" because our minds will be the way of activating it. We set patterns in a mental medium, ours or God's, for God pronounced the word and it still exists in God's mind, therefore it is ever working because the Spirit is ever-present here.

We must come to think of the mental medium, which is the Law governing spiritual mind healing, in terms of exact law. We should think of it as the mind of God. We should not think of it as Spirit alone. The Spirit of God acts through the mental medium automatically, for the Spirit acts as a Self-knowing force. It carries within it the feeling, the personality of the Creator.

Let us consider the idea that God, or reality, is an infinite knower, a limitless doer. We are merely reaffirming the thought that the universe contains the pure spirit and is filled with warmth and color that is the material demonstration of the love of God for the creation. It is illumined through the Christos by the divine presence. It is filled with the divine idea. In other words, we are surrounded by an atmosphere, a presence in the universe that is conscious, alive, awake and aware. We must be conscious that our atmosphere functions the same way.

In this divine presence, we live and move and have our being. This is the medium upon which inspiration, intuition and the three aspects of the Christ – light, life and love – are conveyed to us. It is this presence of God that is the living Spirit, the eternal reality, the Supreme Being with whom we communicate in prayer and meditation. It contains the ever-present, silent, receptive place that is the Akasha, or the soul of God. When we ask a question, it is from this soul that floods through the mind into our brain, or into the Self, that the divine infallible answer is given. It is the achievement of the divine communion of God; this is what we call being.

This is the office of prayer, of intercession of the saints throughout the ages. It is this divine inspiration being transmuted in our vehicle as a voice of the invisible. It is the emanation from the burning bush in the wilderness to which Moses responded. It typifies the unproduced, unproductive, uncultivated place of mind. It is our need met by the consuming fire of love descending from the Creator in heaven.

Moses had gone out into the wilderness to meditate and pray. He was in need of conviction and inspiration. Somehow, in his meditation or prayer, he so completely left the human will behind that God spoke and made itself heard. The pure reality of pure voice, or sound vibration, would be very painful to our physical body. Thus it came through the burning bush that had no personal will of its own. So the most humble event may proclaim the omniscience of God or Good.

The weakest link of any chain of cause and effect may be so tempered by the flame of a new concept that it may have sufficient strength to bind a complete sequence together.

It is necessary that we be careful not to confuse divine presence with the universal Law. The Law is a principle, the immutable cause and effect. As we examine this, we find that the Law is conscious and aware and completely responsive to the creation. The universal mind in its subjective state is what we refer to when we speak of the Law of mind.

One of the most difficult things for us to understand is that while we may consciously definitely direct the Law and set its creative intelligence into motion for good, the Law is not self-conscious. In other words, even though this Law is creative and intelligent, even though it is conscious of our desire, it has no self-consciousness, no self-choice with regard to such a desire. It must execute the directions given to it by our Self-knowing mind. It must respond to our word.

Jesus said, **"Heaven and earth shall pass away, but my Word shall not pass away."** This is a wondrous concept of unity with God and the command of the Law. This shows the difference between a schoolteacher and a teacher. Jesus taught as one having authority, not as one repeating the words of others. This is why the wind and the waves obeyed Him.

We receive the inspiration from the Spirit, but we command the Law. In the common occurrences of our daily lives, we are so accustomed to the reactions of these laws. We never stop to recognize that in using any law of nature, we are dealing with the creative agency that knows what to do and how to do it but cannot have any self-choice. That choice is ours.

In other words, electricity does not know whether it is furnishing motive power to a subway or boiling an egg. When the switch is turned on, in that certain sense, it knows what it should do, what path it should follow, and it must do this. We must decide and choose the pattern. This is why we put copper wires from the source to the equipment that we want the power to move through. It has the authority of the laws of nature but no volition.

It is the energy, but itself remains undirected and subject to our desires, and if this were not true of the laws of nature, we could not depend on them, and we would be confronted with chaos. It is because we can depend on the laws of nature that this is an exact science. It is subject to our conscious use, and it is a principle of nature, just as the laws of affinity in chemistry.

Many times we ask how a prayer can be answered to someone who has no understanding of this Law. But we forget that through pure faith, a person with a great need arrives at a state that would permit the function of this Law. But to reproduce this at will, to reduce it to a laboratory experiment whenever and wherever we desire is a different thing. One is chance, the other science. One is ignorance, the other wisdom. One is the path of the penitent sinner and the other is the way of the true follower of Jesus Christ.

The Law of mind is absolutely impersonal. We might call it the way of the word that works through the mind. Once set into motion, it produces a logical result. It proceeds in a mathematical manner to create, and unless the tendency set in motion is changed, it will create a logical result whatever idea is given to it.

WE CANNOT DESTROY THE LAW BUT WE CAN RE-DIRECT ITS MOVEMENT. In this concept lies the possibility of freedom from bondage, not that we can change the Law, but we can change its direction.

Our spirit has Self-consciousness and Self-choice. The Law, having neither self-consciousness nor self-choice, automatically reacts to the Spirit. Therefore, when we are treating or saying a prayer for someone else, we are really treating ourselves or praying for ourselves. This is exactly the way the Law works. We will never have to go outside ourselves to treat any person, place or thing. To think it necessary to do so would be to deny the unity of God and our access to the universal Law of cause and effect.

Within this one Law, all events transpire. Emerson rightly said that history is the record of the doings of this mind on our planet.

We must remember that the Law of mind is a binding force. It is intelligent. Subconscious does not mean unconscious.

132

Subconscious means below the threshold of conscious mind. As a matter of fact, the subjective laws of the universe that we use in giving treatments have limitless intelligence and limitless power to proceed from cause to effect. It is the creative agency of our universe. When we give a treatment or pray to help someone sick or in need, no matter what the need may be, we must be conscious that we are making a definite statement in the mind and that mind is the sole and only acting agency. The Law acts upon our thought projected into the experience of the one to whom we direct it. The whole mental-spiritual practice is what is meant in the Testament, **"Be still and know that I am God."** It is in back of the illumined thought of Jesus when He said, **"You shall know the truth and the truth shall make you free."**

God is the Trinity, the three in One, having a threefold nature. God is spirit or Self-knowingness; God is Law or action, God is form or result. It is the Trinity that runs through all the religions of the world and it is recognized in all the teachings. We might call it here: the Thing, the Way it Works, and What it Does. This is creation. The law is set in motion and produces what the spirit knows.

God knows no evil. This will help us to have an understanding of the nature of God, which must be truth, beauty, and peace, as God is always in tune with His nature. Because God cannot will evil, we know that it will disappear from our experience in exact proportion to how much we cease using destructive thoughts. Evil is merely a misconception, the wrong way of using good. It is limitation that God knows nothing of, because the nature of God is infinite, and that which is infinite cannot will limitation.

Emerson expressed this beautifully: "The finite alone has wrought and suffered; the infinite lies stretched in smiling repose."

The Law never initiates anything; it always reacts to the spirit. Let us realize that the spirit is both the circumference and the center of everything. There is such a perfect completion within our own souls that we really do have access to the very soul of the universe.

While there is no limit to the Law, there appears to be a limit to our use of it. We said "appears." This means that even though the Law of creating is infinite, we shall draw from it only as much good as our measure will hold – no more, no less. This brings us back to the central theme that God, the universal creative Spirit, creates by Self-knowing or contemplation. We who are in God's image and a copy of the creative Spirit, act in accord with our nature. We create by contemplation or Self-knowingness. This explains the saying of Jesus, **"You shall know the truth and the truth shall make you free."** It is evident that if the knowing of something can produce freedom, there must be a Law that automatically reacts to our knowing.

When we treat or pray for a physical or financial betterment in someone's life, we have to be conscious that their good is now made manifest. To the degree we are aware of this good, it will appear in that person's experience. Becoming aware of their good is an interior awareness. As a result of this Self-recognition, Self-knowing, and Self-consciousness, the Law automatically reacts to it and produces it. Our Self-knowing produces an objective form, a physical condition that exactly equals our mental picture, just as water fills the vessel that contains it.

The Spirit and Law were never created; they co-exist as part of the eternal reality. The Law that we use, the mind that we use, and the Spirit which we are, are all one. Let us consider the fact that there is no such thing as my mind, your mind, his mind or her mind. Mind is an eternal principle in the universe, and when we think, we are making use of it. As we think, we are individualizing it.

Just as all physical nature is made up of one ultimate stuff including our physical bodies, and just as each body is a peculiar individualization of that stuff, so all individual mentalities emerge from one universal mind. We should think of ourselves as being in such complete unity with that mind that there are no longer two, only one. As we think within our being, we think only of being. Mind is the realm of causes; conditions are the realm of effects. New thoughts create new conditions.

There is but one mind, and that mind is the great creative mind. We live and move and have our being in that mind. Each of us uses a part of that great mind and makes it a personalized part for our own use. Therefore we have put a wall around a part of that mind. This is why we feel that we are separated from God until we are in the lower stages of Illumination.

The basis of all energy is in the mind of God as God is in mind.

Romans 8:5-6 **"For they that are after the flesh do mind the things of the flesh, but they that are after the Spirit mind the things of the Spirit. For to be carnally minded is death, but to be spiritually minded is life and peace."**

If we dare to operate in carnal mind, we shall surely die or become separated from God's energy. The spiritual mind is the mind of Christ and is life.

II Timothy 1:7 **"For God has not given us the spirit of fear but of power and love and a sound mind. The awareness of the spirit of a sound mind is given to us by God, through dedication and yielding up all to God."**

II Corinthians 8:12 **"For there be first a willing mind, it is accepted according to what we have and not according to what we have not."**

This teaches us to be of willing mind. Without willingness, nothing can be accomplished. God will not force us to do anything. We must be willing of ourselves to do the will of our Creator. The reference "to mind" is to pay attention to what takes concentration. Using the mind in concentration is the act of giving life to what we are paying attention to. The way this works is that God's energy is the radiation of the mind.

We must exercise the mind constantly for God.

Phillipians 2:5-6 **"Let this mind be in you which is also in Christ Jesus, who being in the form of God thought it not robbery to be equal with God."**

Isaiah 26:3 **"You will keep those in perfect peace whose mind is yielded to the Christ."**

The Christ does the functioning; as this mind will begin to produce the Christ in you.

Mind is an attribute of the soul. The brain is not logically of the body unless we admit that the mind is an attribute of the soul. The human mind cannot be absolutely destroyed with the body. The first phase of soul personality of primitive humans evolved as an image of God. It is also true that our automatic functions of reflex and body type are recorded in the soul.

OUR BIRTH IS BUT A SLEEP AND A FORGETTING, THE SOUL THAT RISES WITH US, OUR LIFE'S STAR, HAS HAD ELSEWHERE ITS SETTING AND COMES FROM AFAR.

MIND II

We reason in two forms: deductively and inductively. Life consists of these two processes of reasoning. One form of reasoning is predominant over the other, whether this is intentional or unintentional. Most reasoning is done by the subjective mind. The experiences of a psychic nature come from the reasoning of the subjective mind. Reasoning in general is the analytical thinking we do. Our conscious reasoning uses the objective mind, while the more important reasoning is done in the subjective mind. When we analyze a statement, we use our ability to reason. If we wanted to know what colors are contained in the color green, we would hold the color green before our mind's eye and examine it. Our reasoning would tell us that green must be composed of both blue and yellow. Such reasoning is analytical. It examines the idea from every angle. It separates the idea into various parts and tries to find the cause. This reasoning leads back to the idea, the thoughts, the actions and principles that preceded the idea with which we began.

If a very fancy cake that looked like a wedding or birthday cake was placed before us on a table, and we were asked to allow our reasoning abilities to influence our actions and thinking, we would do one of two things. We would try to eat some of it, or we would study and examine it. The cause of our action would be found in the type of reasoning we did. If we examined the cake, we would be reasoning inductively. We would note the finish of the cake, trying to guess at the recipe and methods for making the icing. We would imagine the ingredients and the steps that would be taken to make this cake, following along through the various stages. Our reasoning process is from effect back to the cause. We would see the result, the effect, and reason back to the ingredients, the cause. Detectives, when called to solve a murder, look at the dastardly deed, and by reasoning backward are able to tell just how the crime was committed, when and by whom. They

137

go backward, step-by-step, to the cause, and thus have a picture of the actions leading up to the crime. This is inductive reasoning.

Inductive reasoning is progressing from results to causes, step by step, logically. Now if we see the cake and immediately proceed to eat it, we would reason deductively. Our reasoning would be something like this: "That is a fine cake. Cake is good to eat. This one was made to eat. It was made with great care, so it is especially good and palatable. I like cake, and I can enjoy it by eating it. Therefore I will eat this cake." The criminal would walk into a store and see someone counting money. He would reason: "I need money. There is plenty of it. I need some or all of that, so I will take it. The man counting it is protecting it. Therefore I will get rid of the man and take the money. To get rid of him, I will kill him. To kill him I will shoot him in the back with my revolver. He will drop to the floor. He will die. I will take the money and run. I will get out the window. I will have the money. I will be gone."

The criminal would plan every move until the time came to reason differently. He would reason deductively: How the persons would search for him, how the police would be called in, how his fingerprints would be examined, and so forth. He would try to do those things that would defeat their reasoning. Deductive reasoning consists of logical steps forward from the primary idea to its ultimate conclusion.

Most of our reasoning contains a little of both deductive and inductive processes. If we want to make a journey to a distant city, we might reason deductively at first. We would figure out the first move we have to make, the cost of the trip, the time it will take to travel there, the inconvenience of the journey, the place we are going, whom we want to see there, what we are going to do, what it will cost while there, when we will return, and other incidentals of the trip. In other words, we make the trip mentally from start to finish. This is following the idea to its conclusion, deductively.

But if we ask ourselves why we are going there, then we begin to reason inductively. We reason backward to the cause of our taking the trip.

If we always and only reasoned deductively, we would make many mistakes, but at the same time we would accomplish a great many things both good and bad. If we reasoned only deductively, all our acts would be like starting a railroad engine moving forward on its track without an engineer. It would follow the track regardless of all obstacles and keep going to the end of the line. Signals along the way would mean nothing to the engine since the sole aim would be to keep going on the track to the end. It would not stop and examine the signs to see whether it should take a different branch, for that would require inductive reasoning. Also, if we reasoned inductively all the time, we would stay exclusively in a constant process of analysis. We would reason backward to the cause, questioning the causes until we were lost in the fine threads of dim memory with hardly a recollection to the original idea that started the whole process.

God has given us the ability to reason in both ways as a protection so we can progress by means of analyzing our acts and to avoid mistakes. We can reason so that we can make no mistakes. We still make mistakes, so why does this happen? If our reasoning is valid, then why the mistakes?

Logic is either valid or invalid. Science tries to look at the causes but often fails to look at the effect behind the cause. We need to understand the principles of the causes themselves that produce the effects. It is often easier to begin with the created, the effects, rather than the pure principles of creation, which have been neglected and lost to most of us through past ages. Because of our attempted separation from

God's mind, our selfish purposes have blinded us to how things work.

Most reasoning is based on a premise, a statement and a conclusion. It will then be difficult to go astray in our conclusions if our premises are based on truth. We are all a little careless in making our premises, so it is understandable that we arrive at so few valid conclusions.

For example: "Stones sink in water. This thing is a stone. This thing sinks in water."

How simple this reasoning seems and how true, at least by appearances. But suppose our stone was a piece of porous pumice. It is a stone, but it floats. What is wrong? It is our premise that stones sink in water. The stone might be ice, and then it would have to be very heavy to sink and it would take some time. Our premises are usually simple-minded assumptions hardly based upon any laws or facts. Or they are related to facts very obliquely. We have to get back to laws and principles in order to perceive and explain the exact premise of truth.

> **The weakness or strength of deductive reasoning is in the premise.**
> **The weakness or strength of inductive reasoning is in the process.**

There can be no mistakes in the premise or in the process.
"No finite being is exempt from error;
All men are finite beings;
Therefore no man is exempt from error."

The major premise is that no finite being is exempt from error. The minor one is that men are finite beings. So everyone errs. All logic is based on this method. We should try this method of reasoning.

140

Our consciousness of the Law and our ability to demonstrate the supremacy of spiritual thought force over all apparent material resistance must necessarily depend on our understanding of it and how it operates. The Law is the canvas upon which we paint the scene of our lives.

We must come to think of this mental medium or Law – the principle governing spiritual mind control, bringing to us our likes and dislikes – as the foundation of spiritual healing. We must think in terms of this Law as an exact Law that does not vary and does not err. The Law is the mind of God. It was in the Creator when the universe was created. It is in God's mind yesterday, today and forever. The Law is imprinted and is part of the nature of the Spirit of God. It is a facet of God's personality.

This Law functions automatically because the Spirit is Self-knowing and conscious of the things in the mind of God. It causes all mental patterns to be filled with energy because of the Self-knowing of the spirit. God passed on the creative Word to us through our Lord Jesus Christ. Think of God as an infinite knower and a limitless doer. This universe is filled with pure spirit, with warmth and color.

The following are five steps to understanding the function of mind so that it becomes a part of our knowing and use of the Law.

1. DIGESTION – to assimilate mentally; obtain information, ideas or principles; to arrange methodically in the mind; think over; to arrange in convenient order; reduce to a system; classify; to condense, abridge, summarize (Latin, digestus – separated, dissolved).

2. ASSIMILATION – to take in and incorporate as one's own; to bring into conformity; adapt or adjust; to

141

make like; cause to remember; to compare; liken (Latin, assimilatus – likened to; to make like).

3. ASSUMPTION – the act of taking for granted; or supposing; act of taking upon oneself; the act of taking possession of something; the bodily taking up into heaven of the Virgin Mary (Latin, assumptus – taken up).

4. COMPREHENSION – Inclusion; perception or understanding; capacity of the mind to perceive or understand; the act or process of comprehending; to understand the meaning of; grasp with the mind; to take in or embrace; include; comprise (Latin ,to grasp).

5. REALIZATION – Being made real of something imagined; state of being realized; to grasp or understand clearly; to bring vividly to the mind; real-true, not merely ostensible, nominal, or apparent; existing as fact; actual rather than imaginary, ideal, or fictitious; being an actual thing; having an objective existence; genuine, not counterfeit, artificial or imitation; unfeigned or sincere.

These steps are the rungs on the ladder to the higher consciousness of a new life in a new body. These are the way the mind works from the dense to the less dense.

MIND III

Mind: what is it?

Our mind is part of the mind of God into which the sentience and consciousness of the soul arises. The absorption depends on the level of consciousness we express, which determines the sharpness and purity operating in our reasoning. As we grow from childhood, we do not reach the possibility of full consciousness of our level of purity in the mind of God until we are twenty-eight years of age.

The subconscious mind is that portion of the mind that acts below the level of conscious awareness. It is constantly active and never sleeps but continues unfailingly in its operations. Subconscious mind has perfect connection with all points or interims of time and space, and this perfect connection is the basis of telepathy. It is also the Law and the way through which we are put in touch with our spiritual teachers. When the soul has become spiritually effervescent from the activity of the light and the life of Christ within us, then we are ready for instruction by the teachers on the higher level.

Through this medium of mind, we are drawn to those who can teach us. Once our call has been sent out in prayer and meditation and we know the teacher exists, they come into manifestation for us. We are not alone, for our souls and our minds are not isolated. In the inner realm, or the mind of God, all are connected to the one great reality; the one great sentient mind of God. This is how our intuitions reach us from the great mind, passing into consciousness. Instinct comes out of the subconscious itself from the memory of nature and the past memories of the soul.

Because of its retentive nature in the sense of holding vibration and the relative relationship of all that has been or exists now, the Akashic records can be contacted and read by those who have developed it, i.e. by those who have spiritual sight, or who have had the veil removed from the Self. Then we can read past life experiences, even of the many previous lifetimes. This is difficult for most people because it requires complete removal of the mind itself when one is receiving the impressions.

We have in the body the pituitary gland that acts as a transmitting station through which the cosmic thoughts are relayed to the lower centers, where they may be correlated with other experiences. The moon symbolizes the pituitary body because of its reflective nature. It is sometimes pictured as a rolled-up scroll containing all that is written, associated with the element of water because of its psychic reaction.

Picture the subconscious mind as a tilled and fertile field that is every moment receiving seeds dropped from the conscious mind. As we think, speak and visualize, so do we sow and so shall we reap. If we have a feeling or desire attached to our thoughts, the Law of Karma works as surely as the Law of Cause and Effect in action, but more subtly. The world in which we live and move is the result of many words, thoughts and imaged pictures which we carelessly or knowingly drop into the soil of our garden.

It is like an orchard being harvested; some fruit is good and some is not. Dwell on the good and joyful. Emphasize it and magnify it, giving thanks to God continually, not just because the past produced good fruit but so that each thought of thanksgiving – though it brings a kind word today or a rebuff tomorrow – will bear fruit in time. Otherwise the weeds of resentment or the rebuffs will outnumber or outweigh the good seeds.

Our subjective mind only reasons deductively. There is a good purpose behind this for it has one mission in life – to obey orders and to do as it is told or inspired to do by the soul, for it has charge of involuntary actions.

The law of suggestion works through the subconscious, for suggestion is a very subtle command, request, wish or action of law transmitted from the subjective mind to the objective mind. The subjective mind has perfect memory. It is a complete storehouse of facts and experiences, well protected yet easily reached by the consciousness. It is like a vault with separate entrances for every field of knowledge. Each fact enters and leaves by the same door. It is released, as taught in psychology, by a thought that plows a pathway of discharge through the mind by which it ever after tends to escape.

The subconscious mind actually is more impressed with our personality in the last life than by the personality in this new incarnation because the personality of this life is being formed now and much of it is in the blood and the flesh. The word "Akasha" is taken from Sanskrit, meaning "primary substance" or "that out of which all things were and are formed." These Akashic records are maintained in the universal mind and are the forces of the Spirit or universal intelligence that directs the Spirit. Therefore we can say that the Akashic records are the indelible or eternal record of the divine mind, containing all the knowledge of the past, present and future. These are not material records or written accounts but are the divine consciousness of past or future events.

One of the functions of the mind is to use it in concentration by keeping it quiet. Therefore, when we begin to have some degree of consciousness developed, we are establishing a degree of attainment with the universal mind and these Absolute records – the Akasha. The use of intuition is just the first manifestation that such attainment is being established. It is not until we reach a degree of control that the voices of the cosmic, coming through the subconscious, can whisper facts or knowledge through urges that arise within us when we are pondering or in doubt.

When we choose to use the brain and reasoning in any matter, the Cosmic mind, through the subconscious, tries to set us straight. But we have gotten out of the habit of listening until reason gets the upper hand. Now let us put aside reasoning and listen to the still, small Voice until it again becomes automatic and of first importance to hear the reality of truth.

The subconscious mind has ways of collecting obsessive impressions independently of the conscious mind, absorbing impressions of which the conscious mind is not aware. Certain things are not impressed on the ordinary receptors but upon extrasensory nerves that are made to receive higher rates of vibration. By these impressions we pick up things that are carried to the subconscious, bypassing the conscious mind. In such cases the subconscious mind receiving the impressions stores away the pictures or ideas. They remain there, unknown to the conscious mind, until they come across the borderline of the conscious mind and become known for a passing moment. We have a dual consciousness able to communicate with either our conscious or subconscious minds.

The purpose of concentration or meditation is to bring about a borderline condition as the balancing of the two arms of the scale. We may look upon ourselves as being in an arena, around which are numerous doors to cells like monks' cells. In each of these we hold a personality of the past.

As we gain inner consciousness and draw closer to the Akasha, and as our subconscious rises, we sort of visit these alcoves, looking in some we may like and some we may not like, examining particular personalities we had in previous lifetimes. Some might be male, some female. In accordance with these the level of our cosmic consciousness is developed. Until we have acted upon our present life functionally, we depend on past experiences that radiate on the soul because of the light coming through the Self.

Inherent subconscious traits of personality are often inherited from past incarnations. An outstanding trait from which we suffer deeply may be one that took many long, slow years in previous lives to acquire so that it becomes deeply ingrained in us – a part of us. We carry this totally in the soul. Sometimes, as we gain the ability to look into the records of our past, we might observe blank spots signifying absolutely no action at fairly regular intervals. This shows the periods of rest between cycles of material manifestation or incarnation on a material plane, whether it be on the earth or any other planet.

In some ancient writings, the record of the past was symbolized as a rolled-up scroll, representing the entire memory of the person. It is often said that we who become adept may read our history from the Akasha, be it pleasing or not. The subconscious is called subconscious because whatever it does occurs below the level of conscious awareness. It is not on the material plane.

A good exercise to provide an example of what we are saying is to trace back all the words and thoughts of the last half an hour and then read them over carefully and see if we like them. If we don't, strike them out, wipe them out and put a positive thought in their place. Thus the mind will harvest no unfavorable harvest in the future from the subconscious by receiving false or negative ideas. Let's have no garden of weeds for us to harvest.

The mastery of mind is our great objective, and the first step would be to follow Christ and the Master Jesus. Once this is accomplished, we have become masters of our destiny insofar as it is not under certain rational Karma or cosmic trend, and we will be radiating positive seeds among all those we come in contact with.

The subconscious mind is absolutely subordinate to the conscious mind and thus is reactive to reasoning. It is amenable to suggestion and can be controlled. It is of feminine aspect in action, whereas consciousness is masculine. The conscious mind originates and the subconscious creates. The conscious mind makes clear pictures in our minds and thinks positive thoughts. These must outweigh gossip, complaints and elaboration of the dirt someone did to us or the misery we have been feeling. The subconscious mind does not know any better. It has been given the function of creating with the ingredients given to it, and does the job perfectly. Whatever the ingredients given to it, it will give back to us in outer circumstances. We should get out our mental vacuum cleaners and give ourselves a good mental housecleaning, ridding ourselves of all negative thoughts, turning our eyes toward God and towards Christ in the light of the Christos.

In Phillipians 4:6 we read, **"In everything, let your petitions be known to God in prayer and supplications with thanksgiving."** Instead of faultfinding, wait a minute and look for something to praise and give thanks for. Look at each person or thing carefully, magnify them, and soon you will see something to be joyous for. Still more important is the thanksgiving of faith as Jesus, in multiplying the loaves, looked upward and gave thanks before the miracle happened and became an event on the earth. It had already been done in mind and perfect faith in knowing.

In John 6:11 we read how Jesus fed the 5,000 with five loaves of bread and two small fish, **"And Jesus took the loaves; and when He had given thanks, He distributed them to the disciples, and the disciples to them that were sat down;**

148

and likewise of the fish, as much as they wanted." This is the only miracle reported in all four gospels. In the other gospels, the word "blessed" is used in place of "thanks," as used by John. These are some of the tools that we use to keep the mind scrubbed up so that the subconscious is not growing tares in the wheat crop that we have planted for the harvest.

If we live this day and are not resisting the return of the Christ force that is present in the new earth as it is developing, we must keep a positive mind and a clean mind. Unless people of the earth clean out the rubbish in their bodies and minds now, there will be too much for the human body to clean out as the new earth is built. Look around and see the rubbish and waste in the world today, and it will tell us the rubbish that is in the mind of the earth – mass mind.

Let us remind you again: Steady yourself so that you do not react to the negativity of the world or the acts of others. Thus we can go on into the future and not pass through transition now. As a new heaven and the new earth are forming, do not hold any negation or sorrow within; do not water your plants with a few tears occasionally to wash out your emotions. You will be blessed as the positive things grow. This is one reason that you bless them that persecute you and return good for evil. Although some enemy is tossing weed seeds into the garden of your subconscious, the seeds never hit the ground unless your own mind accepts them.

You must not accept what you do not want mentally. If you are living in difficult circumstances, you know those circumstances are not merely material but that you must work all the harder to plant for the future by being Christlike today. There are other areas of the field that will come into fruition tomorrow through grace.

IF YOU WISH TO SOW NEGATIVE SEEDS NOW, YOU WILL PAY LATER.

IF YOU WISH TO SOW POSITIVE SEEDS NOW, YOU WILL REAP THE HARVEST OF USEFUL FRUIT.

FAITH

"If you have faith as a grain of mustard seed, you shall say to this mountain, be removed to yonder place, and it shall be removed, and nothing shall be impossible to you."

In the Bible, the word "faith" is used many times, and in some religious circles today it is just a word. But faith is something that is real. It is not just a word. When we have faith in God, that means we stop talking and start doing.

In business or the stock market we may take a look at various companies and will decide which one will be the best one to invest in. We have faith in that company because we put our money where our hope is.

When we have faith that we can heal, we start putting our hands on people and ask for healing either by direct contact or using the Word and mind. Faith is an action word. Without faith we could not move a muscle. A newborn baby learns how to walk through faith. As a baby, we see others around us walking and telling us we can walk too. By faith, we stand on our feet and put one foot in front of the other. We may stumble and fall a few times, but we do walk. If we had sat and thought within ourselves, "I wonder if I can do this?" We would have been sitting there for 90 years wondering if we could do it. When we have faith, it means that we'll get up and try doing that which is there to do and we will keep right on trying until we succeed.

The term "faith" exists because most of the world we live in is unseen, and it will remain unseen until we step out in faith. Then the unseen will be seen for us. This seen world is just the effect of the unseen world. The reality isn't in the seen world but in the unseen. The only reason it is unseen is because we have lost the consciousness of God, and the greater part of God's being is in the unseen world.

151

Something may be unseen, but if we take a step it will then appear, and the taking of that step is faith. This whole physical world moves and runs on faith. When we make a contract to buy a home, we have stepped out on the faith that we will keep our job that will let us bring in the money to make the payments each month.

The term unseen world doesn't mean unreal world. It just means that it isn't apparent to those who haven't developed the full range of sight. The unseen world is as much "here and real" as the seen world. The difference between the unseen and the seen is that in the unseen is the source of all power.

Faith is not what the churches teach. It is the knowing that the Law works and that the Word works. Faith is knowing without knowledge, acceptance without reason, and action without definition of the cause. Faith is not accidental but is developed.

The act of faith unleashes tremendous power into action. It is not made up of blind beliefs or hopes. It is the act of knowing that what we ask is now, or is going to be done, and that the prayer will be answered. Faith starts with an assumption. We assume the existence of something, like we assume our cars are insured. Likewise, we assume the truth about God, and expect the Creator to take care of us, as when we were little children.

Faith is the assuming that precedes knowing, that precedes realization, in the triangle, action from faith. Faith is knowing we are right, because we have to know that much. Matthew talked about the manna of God in 6:30, **"But if God so clothes the grass of the field, which today is alive and tomorrow is cast into the oven, will God not much more clothe you, oh you of little faith?"** Here we see that even the grass has a pattern set by God. It is provided for. This shows the unlimited power of human beings through the power of

God and the tool of faith. Jesus said in Matthew 21:22 that whatsoever you ask in prayer, you will receive, if you have faith.

In Mark 11:24, Jesus said, **"Whatsoever you ask in prayer, believe that it is being done and it will be."** We have a definite lead to the lesson on the Law. You are to believe that you have already received what you ask because you have set the pattern in the mind of God.

In the story of the woman who touched the hem of Jesus' garment, Jesus said, **"Take heart, daughter. Your faith has made you well."** Here, we see that we need to have a feeling with our faith, especially when we are dealing with the physical body. In Acts 3:16, Peter says, **"Faith in his name has made this man strong whom you see and know; and the faith which is through Jesus has given this man perfect health in the presence of you all."**

In Thessalonians 5:8, **"But since we belong to the day, let us be sober and put on the breastplate of faith and love, and for a helmet the Hope of Salvation."** This is the knowing that nothing may touch us when we have faith that we are protected.

Hebrews 11:1, **"Faith is assurance of things hoped for, the conviction of things not seen."** The word "assurance" is a felt guarantee of performance. In the word "conviction," we have the knowing of its reality.

Hebrews 12:2, **"Looking to Jesus who was the pioneer and perfecter of our faith for the joy that was set before Him, who endured the cross despising the shame and is seated at the right hand of the throne of God."** This is the explanation of what was accomplished on the cross in the way of perfecting our faith through his death and resurrection, or a seen performance. Hebrews 11:3, **"For by faith we** understand how the world was created by the Word of God, so that what is seen was made of things which do not appear." Here, we are told that what appears in the dense world is made out of the substance of the unseen world.

Faith is a most important spiritual teaching. The dictionary defines it as: To trust or to confide in; unquestioning belief in God; anything believed; childlike reliance. But we have seen a deeper understanding. **"Faith is the substance of things hoped for..."** Substance is the real or essential part of anything, essence, reality or matter. It is something that has independent existence and is acted upon by causes and events. Faith is that which creates a condition of being evident, a realistic sign that tends to prove ground for belief, indication or sign. We can see the normal church teachings on faith are lacking this depth. Here is our understanding of faith: It is that which is real or essential. It exists independently of our senses, and is acted upon by causes and events.

In II Timothy 4, Paul says he has kept the faith, meaning that he was faithful to the substantial reality of the Christ. **"And He said to them, 'Why are you afraid, O men of little faith?'"** In Romans 1:5, **"...grace is given for obedience in faith, or with faith."**

In Galatians 2, we find that we live by faith in the Son of God. In Romans 10:8 we find that we preach the word of faith, or in essence, the word of substance or reality. Paul further tells us that what is not faith, is sin. If it is not real or substantial – if it is not self-evident or essential – it is sinful, or a transgression of the Law that states that all things truly spiritual are self-evident, eternal and realistic.

We find out what actually happens to us when we continue in the faith by reading Colossians 1:23, **"And you who were once estranged and hostile in mind, doing evil deeds. He** has now reconciled in his body of flesh by his death, in order to present you holy, and blameless, and irreproachable before Him, provided that you continue in the faith, stable and steadfast, not shifting from the hope of the Gospel which you heard, that has been preached to every creature under heaven, and of which I, Paul, became a minister."

We have been told that faith is essential to our salvation. Let us say that faith and confidence are the reality of our salvation. It is one of the many vehicles through which the great light of the Christ travels. When we have true faith, it is solid and substantial. It is so real that we can feel it and see it with our spiritual senses. It is sometimes so real that it will manifest physically, and our faith in it is so evident that no person or beast can deny it.

A speck of belief, such as faith that Jesus Christ can appear to us, gives Him a point of entry and a place whereon to build up his presence and his image. The tiny speck of a seed of faith at the point of beginning grows to great proportion. If we only believe the outer appearances of things as final, then we would have no inner development.

AWAKENING I

"I am the Way, the Truth, and the Life," said Jesus.

All religions, arts and sciences are branches of the same tree. The aspiration of each of us is basically directed to the ennobling of ourselves in whatever profession. Our striving lifts us up to a better experience and existence. Slowly, but surely, we are led toward the reality of what has been recommended: "Man, Know Thyself."

It is not by chance that our present educational system has developed out of the ancient mystery schools. The sciences were first known by the old mystics and spiritual teachers. It would be quite wonderful if both churches and universities sought to prepare people to stand on their own two feet as a counterpart of the great creative mind and power.

As we look at our sisters and brothers, we see some people who stand out in the ranks of humanity as having something that the rest of the masses do not possess. It is the calmness of the person that is the one thing that attracts people to them. They have this gentle attitude, knowing themselves and the power they possess. Some of the teachers are called mystics, some philosophers, but there is something these beings have that seems to endow them with spiritual abilities that others do not have.

This apparent difference was not an inequality of God's doing but rather that they earned this endowment by working with the Law and order of things and abiding by the laws of creation. Actually these people are so close to nature and themselves that they are, in reality, natural scientists. Then we have the lamas, the swamis, the priests and disciples; and let us not forget the apostles of our Masters Jesus and Mary. All are alike in that they had made up their minds that the way of attaining and manifesting the perfection of God was of greater importance than anything else in their lives. They came to the great realization that only when they were able to find God or the understanding of the great creative intelligence would they be able to help other people who had not come to the point of awakening.

We take the mystery out of the mysteries in this new age as they were taught by Jesus, Buddha, and many others. With insight and direct revelation of our Master Jesus Christ and Mother Mary, we not only teach but practice the reality of these teachings. We have realized that level of consciousness and vibration that brings to light the commandments in their reality and a realization of the one way, or the universality in everyone's soul growth.

The awakening to the reality of the way makes it possible for us to function without dogma, without creed, regardless of our affiliation with a group, church or order. The mystical body of Christ exists and relies on the infinite information of the Self and the Law of God. This directs us, regardless of our position on the golden stairway.

It is through our becoming acquainted with the tools of God and how to use them that we are able to work with anyone and sense and see the existence of the greater light. We are conscious of the way that is the ultimate path of attainment that we must travel to peace so that all the world may have peace.

This is the way traveled by the great ones. On this path we find no differentiation in race, creed or color. The path is long and becomes very narrow the further we travel along it. It is also very satisfying. It brings inner peace and security regardless of the turmoil and strife around us.

We have no new philosophy, except to unite ourselves with everyone, as it is our only wish and striving to put these tools of the great Creator into the hands of each sister and brother on earth, and to work with the great White Brother /Sisterhood in bringing the earth in its entirety into the light of the Christos. To be a real sister or brother is to be under the direct guidance of a teacher. Our striving is to understand one another and not just agree to be sociable or at peace.

One of the first rules, if we wish to put our feet on this way, is: don't try to convert a person to our philosophy or religion, but try to understand their philosophy or religion. But do all things in service for our fellow human beings that will help to raise them to our level of appreciation of God. Remember, we only learn to know ourselves by knowing the Creator we live in; working with It, walking the face of the earth without fear or want and in joy and gladness. This is how we can serve God and people.

It takes a brave person to work in the body of Christ and to live God's way. Grow with our Father and with us in this age of beauty and share the glory of the Christos returned to earth. It takes courage to attain our Godhood.

We started out on the path of involution into dense matter. We are now evolving out of dense matter to attain mastery and Godhood. Set your face to the sun; never run; use spear of mind, which is thought to stop what negativity has wrought; be a sister or brother; help another.

The most important event in a spiritual person's life is the awakening of the soul.

In the dictionary, "awakening" means: A waking up, an arousing or reviving, as of impulses or religions. Since a revival is indicated, something must be there that was awake but now sleeps.

Mark 4:38 "**They awoke Jesus and said to Him, 'Master, don't you care that we are drowning?'**" This is the awaking of fear. Jesus rebuked them for their unbelief.

In Luke 9:32, we find the awaking to the Glory of God. "**But Peter and his companions had been overcome by sleep, and it was as they struggled in wakefulness that they saw the glory of Jesus and the two men standing with Him.**"

It is in awakening to the fact that all around us the mass mind is asleep, and that it has lulled us into sleep. We are righteously angered enough into awaking to see the glory of Jesus, which is the glory of God. Jesus reflects God's glory.

John 11:11, "**Our friend Lazarus has fallen sleep, but I am going to wake him up.**" We need to be awakened to the Christ.

"**Awake, O sleeper, and arise from the dead, and Christ shall give you light.**"

Before we may go forth and serve others, the spiritual part of us must be born. It has lain dormant for centuries within us, alive and developing, but not delivered. First we are spiritually children, and then we grow into adulthood to serve with Christ. As Jesus said, "**Behold, I stand at the door and knock.**" We should think of the Lord coming with a flashlight to the door of our temple, and knocking to awaken us, saying: "Turn on your light within the temple, so you may see to rise. Then, when you are fully prepared, I shall return to pick you up to come and help Me."

As Peter said, "**You will do well to pay attention to this as to a lamp shining in a dark place, until the day dawns and the morning star rises in your hearts.**"

The divine child, the son or daughter of God, is born within us in one of our rounds of incarnation, when our consciousness has lifted and we have become amenable to and capable of functioning in righteousness and selfless love. When we have arrived at the capacity to serve God with utter devotion, we will be born to self-forgetting service to all. The more single our eye, the less we look sidewise at the physical life we have stepped out from, the more pure our motives are, the more will we develop the light of the sun within.

God becomes the universe, the blue sky, in which the golden sun-son swims and functions. We are then immersed in God and dwell in God. Collected together in us will be innumerable particles of light that are as invisible as the great Spirit, being all-pervading. But when we gather together in one strong focal point of force and energy, we become the warm strong light around which the lesser beings gather, to whom they look for strength and guidance, the true sons and daughters of God.

The child is born in the very Bethlehem area of our bodies, in the approximate area ruled by Cancer (plus Gemini and Leo). In the zodiacal sign of Cancer is a configuration called the manger. This is to say that the Self is located near the heart area, or behind it, near the spine. It is as though, speaking imaginatively, the twins of Gemini, Adam and Eve, in their home nest of Cancer, became parents as they gave birth to the divine child, the sun, corresponding to the sign of Leo, which rules children and is ruled by the sun, astrologically.

Paul Foster Case said: "Spiritual consciousness is an awakening to the meaning of what material consciousness supposes to be – nothing but physical existence. It is a recognition of the spiritual substance of this world, which ignorance calls matter. The wisdom that results from new birth shows us that we are truly children of the sun, even now. When this knowledge comes, it wells up in our hearts as a song of joy, and we turn from the limitations of the senses to the freedom of spiritual knowing."

Malachi 4:1-2 **"For behold, the day comes, burning like an oven, when all the arrogant and all evildoers will be stubble; the day that comes shall burn them up, says the Lord of hosts, so that it will leave them neither root nor branch. But for you who fear my Name, the Sun of Righteousness shall rise, with healing in its wings."** When the sun comes, and when the Christ's Spirit returns to earth, it will be so dazzling as to destroy all the darkness. It will burn the dross, and only the gold, the righteous, will remain.

When the Christ Spirit comes to show us the way, by its very brightness, the negative shows up the more prominently, as the brighter the light, the darker and more defined is the shadow cast by the object. If we place a light within our bodies so strong that it makes all transparent except that which is foreign to its inherent nature, or that which was not good; the evil tendencies will show up the stronger and have to be faced. There will be no nice, dense place to hide the faults.

As long as there was no light, people could hide their sins. But now our sins show, and we have to get rid of them, or leave the scene. On the other hand, to those who love God, and want to do well, and turn to Christ, this merciless spotlight becomes the healing Sun of Righteousness.

Just so, a teacher, who comes to emulate Jesus Christ on earth, to bring us to the light and to our Creator, has to first flush all our negation to the surface, where it can be gotten rid of, before the teacher can work with the true son/daughter within us. The teacher has to rout out all the anger and hatred and dissipation, the lies and the stealing. The teacher has to make the student face them and consciously turn from all attachment to them.

Jesus healed many people and performed many miracles. He woke Lazarus from the sleep of death, in order that the faith of many might be strengthened. The first real awakening of the soul may come through a "baptism of waters," a cleansing of old sins, initiated by the religious ritual, but accomplished by a shower of life experiences.

Paul promised that the Christ would wake us all when He comes, in Corinthians 15:51, **"Listen! I tell you a mystery. We shall not all sleep, but we shall all be changed, in a moment, in the twinkling of an eye, at the last trumpet. For the trumpet will sound, and the dead will be raised imperishable, and we shall all be changed."**

Some people awake and find their soul empty. Isaiah 29:8 **"But he awakes and his love is empty, but he awakes and he is faint."** Ephesians 5:14 **"Awake you who sleep, and arise from the dead, and Christ shall give you light."** After the great awakening, the light of Christ comes. Nothing can progress spiritually for us until we are awakened by the Christ through the light of his Word in us.

Acts 16:27 **"When the jailer awoke and saw that the doors of the prison had been opened, he drew his sword and was on the point of killing himself."** The jailer is mass mind. When the mass mind sees the arousing of the believer, it will destroy itself.

Romans 13:2 **"Because as I think you have realized, the present time is of the highest importance, it is time to wake up to reality. Every day brings God's Salvation nearer."**

AWAKENING II

Once, when my alarm clock had accidentally not been set, at the precise hour of the early morning when it should have rung, a soft voice whispered my name, and I awoke, in time to get a new job. There was no one else in the house, physically. Perhaps a friendly being decided to give a helping hand, or perhaps my own inner Self intervened.

When it is time for the spiritual awakening, no alarm has been set. But in God's realm of consciousness, it is known that this soul has slept long enough. There is work to be done, and unless we wake to the realization of this, some brother or sister in the higher realm of Spirit may gently nudge us into awakening. Our spirit was born of God originally. As we became more and more engrossed in physical activity and worldly interests, God seemed farther and farther away, until we may have claimed not to believe there was a God at all. Else why all the suffering and sin on the earth plane?

God made us in God's own Image. Surely God never sleeps. Yet we have spent one third of our life physically asleep, and almost all of it spiritually asleep. We wake up a little on Sunday, if we go to church. We lift up our hearts to God when we see the stars, or hear a bird, or find a blossom in spring. We glimpse God in a baby's eyes, and assume some of the Creator's quality in an act of selfless love. Otherwise, most of the time we sleep, except when we get a serious problem. Then we wake up to the hope that God may and must hear us, must help us.

Adam first slept in the Bible when God caused a deep sleep to fall on him while God removed a rib in order to create his mate from his own flesh. This was done so that they might truly be one and not separate entities in nature. Adam woke to find himself with a beautiful wife, Eve. She must have given him great joy, but she also diverted him from his one-pointed attention to God.

Attention can only serve one master at a time. If we are giving whole-hearted attention to providing all the things needed to pre-serve and to serve our bodies, how can we be thinking of God?

Our spiritual awakening must be to the realization of God as a reality. We must acknowledge the creator in all we do. We must keep in remembrance the first Commandment: **"You shall love the Lord your God with all your heart, and soul, and mind, and you shall have no other gods before God."** We awaken to the fact that God really is, and always has been, and always will be. God is more than a being who once created the earth and everything else, talked with us for a while, and then got distracted. God sent down Jesus and Mary in a final gesture to salvage whomever would listen and believe they came from God, and then went into retirement, letting us learn of the Creator's history from books.

When spiritual awakening comes, we know without being told that not only does God live now, continuously, everywhere, but that the Creator loves us, almost beyond imagining, even to the point where God is willing to accept us as sons/daughters (by adoption, as Paul said). God chooses us, when God feels we are ready. When we are reborn to a new consciousness of the great One, and a certainty that we have been given a chance to dwell with God forever, we also know that God expects us to measure up as good children, as inheritors of God's grace. Then we must accept the commission to represent this great Being.

God is mind, the totality of mind, where all things are created. To reach this Being, we must elevate our own minds to something approaching that consciousness, else how can God reach us? We must move very close, dropping away the

166

earthly attentions, the concentration on those things that are below us in the sphere of creation. We have to reach above, as high as we can reach – and that means within as far as we can go, paradoxically. We move within, to the point of absolute zero, past all that can be seen or imagined. There is God.

In all action, refer first to God. Go to sleep thinking of God, and on awakening in the morning, present your mind to God, letting God take it over, and thus become a co-operator with God in all you do. When you think mean or ugly thoughts, you are separating yourself from God's presence, and heading for trouble on a downward path. If you can give up concentrating on that meanness, and surrender all your thinking to God, we will eventually become worthy. God yearns for you to be worthy, worthy to be co-creators with God, having conquered your own mind.

To start all things with God is like starting at the top of the ladder, but we have to place our minds at the top, or our feet will never know enough to start climbing, much less reach the top. We are gods of our own universe. Until we awake within our own minds and inmost beings, how can we wake up the dormant faculties within us? How can we move inert matter, or stir the consciousness of lower stages of life from their comparative stupor into living function?

Psalm 139:18 **"When I awake, I am still with You."** The night is gone, and the new day is almost dawned. We must wake to the fact that we are living in a new age, one that has never appeared on the earth plane before. The New Jerusalem is coming down from God today, not tomorrow. The words of John the Baptist ring true today, **"Prepare the way of the Lord. Make straight God's Path."** The great preparation can only take place after the awakening of the Self into full Realization.

Asleep in the deep are those steeped in the waves of one phase of Neptune's illusions. The psychic waters are attributed to Neptune, and many a channeler or medium seems content to remain submerged in the shimmering semi-realities, which are sometimes true and often quite misleading. Entities who have left the body to pass beyond dwell in this region, as well as the thought forms that have taken form and are now filling with substance, prior to appearing physically.

Some people have slept the sleep of Neptune via drugs or alcohol. Some enjoy it in nightclubs or other glamour spots, where they are drawn by the rhythmic music, the colors, bright lights, and the glamour of persons putting on the evening's glittering personalities. The sleep that comes from using alcohol is commonly known. Any wino asking for the price of a bottle is so sadly asleep, only the most intense desire or motivation can inspire her to wake from the dreary nightmare of her existence, to cease from the false sleep by which she seeks to escape. Many of these people will perish in their self-induced sleep, to wake elsewhere, another day.

But for those who are ready and eager to awaken from the sleep of earth's hold on them, into the higher spiritual realities, the psychic waters act as a medium through which the spiritual beings may act to reach through to the physical, to bring about the awakening. This is the meeting ground, where the spiritual may reach down, and our psychic body may reach up to meet the spiritual, and gain thereby. By means of the psychic world and its energies, discarnate teachers may cause phenomena that aids in teaching an aspirant, or in bringing her to an earthly teacher.

We are aided in this way before we have gained our inner sight or hearing. These teachers bring to us from the outside many lessons or eye-opening experiences, which later we will not need when we gain our spiritual sight and hearing. In

168

Solomon's Song 5:2, we read, **"I slept, but my heart was awake: Hark, my beloved is knocking."** God knocks when the body is asleep but the desire for God awakes. Later, God expects us to be awake, expecting Him.

Water conducts electricity, and the planet Uranus is the great awakener. Uranus rules electricity. In that sense, awakening comes out of the water, like the heavenly waters, as lightning comes out of a thunderstorm. Lightning represents truth, spiritual truth. **"As the lightning flashes from the East even to the West, so shall the coming of the Son of Man be."**

If strange things happen that can hardly be explained by ordinary means, it may well be the gathering of the waters of the heavens through which the lightning of truth will flash to us, and nothing will ever again be the same, for the Spirit of Christ shall have arrived in our consciousness.

Awakening comes to us when processes, actions and desires of the physical body, both mental and emotional, have reached a point where we recognize total failure. This is the time when awakening comes. Our whole body cries out; nothing we have can satisfy that great ache within us, the great vacuum. Words and books will stand for nothing. In conquering death, life begins. As Jesus did.

Every winter, trees seem to die, giving up their robe of green and enduring bitter, crackling cold, until the warm sun of spring appears, when sap stirs in their roots, and soon begins to flow upward to their topmost branches, bringing a beautiful return to full life. With the warm sun of spring, the whole world wakes. Again, speaking astrologically, the first day of spring occurs when the sun enters the sign of Aries, where it is at its place of exaltation. It is also a sign that energizes and acts. Is it any wonder then that the water which had been frozen and held in abeyance all winter on the mountain tops, begins to thaw and tumble down the mountain sides, to fill the brooks and water the fields and valleys below? In the same way, the coming of the Sun of Christ at the dawn of the spiritual awakening within us, melts the long-frozen stream of consciousness within us so that it feeds the seedlings of new spiritual fruitfulness.

AWAKENING III

In waking we emerge from the corridors of sleep. Consciousness comes out from the dark places. In sleep, the body is there, alive but quiescent. The consciousness is somewhere alive, but the two are not functioning together. It is when the bodies all unite, when the reasoning mind, and the body and all the rest come together – all in one place – then do we awake.

In sleep the eyes are closed to outside things. The first proof of waking is the opening of the eyes. The first proof of the spirit awakening is the seeing with new eyes, so that all the things seen before now look new and different. Ordinary humanity is in a deep sleep. We came down from God and entered into the house of our body and became heavily involved with its needs and desires. In serving the temple, rather than the indwelling Spirit, we are walled in by thick flesh and have fallen asleep.

The body needs food, water and shelter. It needs a place to rest. In our primitive state we worked at supplying all these things, and little more. They are essential to the physical upkeep of the vehicle, or to the maintenance of the house. Today we have acquired unnatural tastes, and have to work harder to supply these complex wants. So we keep in a dither doing many things, and become involved in a tangle of bills, jobs and charge accounts.

It is time somebody told us it's morning. Christ is returning and the energy of the sun is pouring into our beings. Let's arise and use this energy, stir ourselves and do something to feed the Spirit that dwells in the temple, as well as the cells which comprise its walls.

Bears go into hibernation in winter to escape the snow and a long period of cold, but they come out as the sun grows warm in spring, along with the crocuses, tulips and baby chicks. The whole symbolism of Easter and spring refers to the awakening of the earth and its creatures to the return of the sun's warmth. A similar expectation is the annual entombment and resurrection of Jesus, demonstrating mastery over all the material elements of creation.

The awakening of our consciousness to God-Realization, as the awakening of the seed below the earth, begins below the level of conscious awareness. It stirs deep down in the subconscious realms of mind and being, just as when we are still asleep, toward morning, certain sounds or movements bring us almost awake, yet drowsiness still holds a curtain about us. It may take an earthquake to rend that veil of the temple, an inner jolt, with the accompanying flash of realization of God's truth. That's the alarm clock of the Spirit.

It may be hard to topple out of bed. But once out, we begin to bloom as a fragrant daffodil in the early morning sun. Birds begin to sing in the flowering trees, and we come outside to breathe the wonderful scent, and yawn, or breathe deeply to take in more of the oxygen of God's own life-breath, the pure air.

After having spent the winter in gestation, animals come forth from the womb to frolic on the spring meadows. The seed unfurls its embryo to push up and show itself above ground just like the baby bird pecks its way out of the enclosing shell. So our locked-in spirits will burst the casement as the solar energies within us get rid of the dross, and open our eyes to the true nature of our beings.

We live by being awake. Being asleep is like existing only in nature, bound by time processes. But awaking is a miracle of God, which ignores time, and takes on eternity. Awake and living, we choose and act freely to change our own destiny. Rocks and minerals apparently sleep, in their slowness of movement. We are the most awake of all creatures because of our high intellects.

In the dictionary, "sleep" is a state of reduced physical and nervous activity, accompanied by the suspension of voluntary movements, and a complete or partial unconsciousness; to be dormant, inactive. "Wake" means to emerge from sleep; to become active or alert, after being inactive or dormant; to keep watch or guard at night; to rouse, stir up, or excite.

All the waking of earth corresponds to the timing of the sun (except for certain night creatures that use night as cover). So does the waking of the Spirit of human beings correspond to the coming of the Christ or Son of God consciousness to our being. We are being reborn to this state through grace.

Isaiah said, **"Your dead shall live, their bodies shall rise. O dwellers in the dust, Awake and sing for joy! For your dew is a dew of light, and on the land of the shades you will let it fall."**

Paul wrote in Thessalonians 5:6, **"But you are not in darkness, brethren, for that day to surprise you like a thief. For you are all sons and daughters of light and sons and daughters of the day. We are not of the night or of the darkness. So let us not sleep, as others do, but let us keep awake and be sober. For those who sleep, sleep at night...; but since we belong to the day, let us be sober, and put on the breastplate of faith and love and... for God...who died for us, so that whether we wake or sleep, we might live with God."**

The Way, the Truth and the Life is the path to eternal peace. There is nothing in the pattern of creation about Catholic, Protestant or Judaism. All of these are the creation of our egos but are and have been used for our advancement. There is, however, in the plan of creation, a set of steps that we must climb if we are going to lift ourselves by our bootstraps. These steps are related to the set of tools that God gave us so that we might attain Godhood.

When we look very closely at the universal picture, we find that our universal tools and the Law are closely related to the various religions. The principle religions are: Buddhism, Christianity, Hinduism, Islam, Judaism, Taoism, and Confucianism. There are over 36,000 Christian denominations in the world. Each of these teach some truths which are helpful to people. But the true Way is universal, and those who follow it can see the unity within all religions and the truth they represent. The real experience of God erases all of these local and national boundaries. One who really has the experience of God is able to recognize it in someone else, whatever their background.

Let us look at the invisible tools that the Creator gave us: Symbolism, Power, Communication, the Law, the Way, Grace, and the Universal Vehicle. The "Staff" spoken of in the 23rd Psalm is the Nameless One and the Universal Vehicle.

In the beginning, a Nameless Wanderer was a Being (Human), all perfect, all sufficient, because we have all the tools, wisdom and power working perfectly. So poised, so balanced that it excluded all else; because it was All. And none but its own Self could comprehend All that it was; in its personal universe, it was ALL.

For God was unknown and unknowable. It was in poise and balance. There was no resistance, no seeking. Its comprehension was infinite. It is a great splendor, majesty, magnificence and all power – and it is the Self. Once found, this is the Master Being. To understand Self is more than the mind can understand, but we may understand our divine obligation and relationship to all functioning, moving form and forces. In all the splendor and majesty and power, this is more than the mind can understand. Only the Self can conceive this.

Then, the Word took flesh and became human, the Christ-Being, the God-Man in all perfection, magnificence and power. The Word was God and God understood who It was, and this realization made It humble. Thus the Word was God, God in great humility and power, for God conceived of Itself. It evolved through Law into the fleshly body of the little child. The child knew the parent but could not understand God, but this was not necessary. All they needed to know was themselves – or Self.

For the Word was given to the Son, and Jesus Christ gave it to us again. We had the Word, and thus the mystery of Genesis unfolded.

Then we gradually forgot one aspect of our nature through working on one of the other aspects of force made prominent in our consciousness due to the influence of the electromagnetic fields of other planets and in relation to the place in this solar system in which that particular birth took place. There we forgot the Creator, or the Father.

Slowly, but surely, as these suns were being created, recreated from the great One, they gradually lost the memory of the original creator. The vagueness of the memory changed their consciousness, breaking down the oneness with the Creator. The created forms became less and less infused with the effluent life, and certain parts of the beings became less active and therefore, internal formations became apparent.

There also began a lonesomeness in the beings due to the crystallization of the spirit; they were becoming denser matter. There was a longing to draw closer to the source of life, to increase their electrical potential, and eventually, from this longing, prayer developed. With the difference of density came knowledge and sensation, for as this creation sensed a difference in the reaction of the spirit in its own universe, it realized how knowledge was revealed. The transfer took place before the expulsion of the New Son was required to take place into the space around it.

Our purpose is to promote a priestly humanity under the Order of Melchizedek, given in revelation as a divine fulfillment and instrument of the Order of the Golden Cross. Its purpose is to coalesce the teachings of Jesus Christ as given in the four gospels of the New Testament with the teachings of all religions and people of the earth by instructing teachers and ministers in the understanding of the Testament and the use of the sacraments.

THE RETURN

All the spiritual teachings on earth have taught the Way. These instructions agree that we must control our minds and desires so that we may cut away the outer to reach the inner – our true beings. The eternal part of us is free of all negation and knows the creation as the Creator created it. The Return is the return to our real being, the original state of being in all power and glory with the Great One. Cutting away the dross gets rid of the desires that hold and confine us to the earth. When we break free of these limitations, we become free beings, sons or daughters who have returned.

The New Testament talks about the prodigal son who was lost and who returned. He sold all of his inheritance and became a slave to the world, to worldly desires. Then he saw that the servants of his father had a better life than he, so he turned his face from all the muck and mire. He started walking back to his father's house. When he was almost there, his father ran to him and brought him the rest of the way and gave him all the treasures of his kingdom.

Jesus was the first of many who have returned. He showed us this inner road and how to rid ourselves of our own blocks.

Many religions have taught the outward appearances of the spiritual path but have failed to teach the great path within, the eternal path of raising ourselves through service to our Creator. The Return is not an abnormal state of being; for once the son or daughter returns to the Father God, then they are living a normal life. This was the pattern since the beginning and is now and ever shall be.

When we look away from this world, from our likes and dislikes, from our opinions and beliefs, and begin to accept things just the way they are, without dogma or interpretation, we are returning to the realness of ourselves and of God. The teachings of Jesus Christ are within us in their totality. This is why Jesus says the "Return" implies that we were there to begin with. For we cannot return to a place we have never been; so the process of returning is remembering that which we already are and where we came from.

The return has no labels; that is to say, no "isms." The return is not a religion, but it is a return to our original greatness. Many people get hung up with beautiful words and catchy phrases. Some call themselves Yogis, Buddhists, Christians and what-not; but when a great Nameless Being created us in its image, what could our name be but just a Nameless Wanderer moving from one existence to another, seeking to find a place where we fit in. When we have returned, we will find that place is within our beings, the Self – or being just what we are.

As we travel through this world, we cling to it, to all the shiny things of the world, trying to grab for ourselves something to call our own. We wind up losing it all when it is time to leave. The only thing we leave with is ourselves – that which we tried to run away from for so long.

The Return is a great reality; for Jesus did not come to earth spouting theology. He told us just what is. He had been there and He knew and experienced it, and He lived in it every day of his life. Even so, He was no freak. He was just like us, except that He had "let go" of everything – including Himself.

When we take God seriously and not as a beautiful idealism, or a beautiful concept, but really seek to find the truth, then we shall return. Until we accept the reality of what Jesus taught, we will roll in the muck and mire of our own making and our own avoidance of ourselves.

Ever since our entrance into life, we have been preparing to return to God. St. Paul says in Romans,

"All have sinned and fallen short of the glory of God."
Since the fall of Adam and Eve, we have lost control over the universe, which was given to us by the Creator at the beginning of creation. It is this power and authority, this son/daughtership that we are returning to. This is our inheritance that we sold.

In the Prodigal Son story, the younger son asked his father for a share of all his property, and the father complied with this request. It was not long before the child went off to a foreign land and squandered all he had. When he had run out of his inheritance, a famine broke out in the land, and the son began to feel it. He hired himself out to a citizen of that land who put him in charge of feeding the pigs. He began to be hungry and fed himself on the slop the pigs ate. He came to a great awakening and realized that his father's servants lived a better existence than he did.

In deep humility he returned home and made a plea before his father to accept him back as a servant only. The father welcomed him back with open arms, and restored him to his rightful place, putting the ring of authority on his finger. His brother was extremely jealous, and complained to his father about his younger brother. The father replied that the son who stayed was with him always, and for this he was grateful. But the younger brother was like a dead man who had come to life, and that he was lost and now had returned. With great festivity and music, the father had accepted the return of the wayward son.

One of the great lessons that we learn when we go through the great awakening is that we have been separated from our Creator through subjecting ourselves to God's creation, and have wasted our divine inheritance as children of the Creator. We lost this inheritance through misuse of power, lack of understanding of the Law, and stubbornness towards God's will. This is the way we have sinned.

We were created to be heirs with God, and joint heirs with Christ, to have dominion over the things of this world. The things of the world are to be fully under our control. The two sons of the father in the story symbolize an old order and a new order. The old order has been with God from the beginning. The new order is alive and coming into fulfillment.

The old order refused to die out and make way for that which is coming into full manifestation. The old order is controlled completely by mass mind, which speaks to it of its own self-righteousness in keeping former laws and regulations established by the Creator for a time and a season. Mass mind refuses to allow the old order to realize the time is at hand for a transition, a complete change. Therefore the mass mind is compelling the old order to transgress the law of God. The sons of God, symbolized by the prodigal son, have come through this old order, and are defying it. At one time we even defied the very will of the Creator. Now we are returning to the Creator's house in order to fulfill our mission as masters of this earth under Jesus Christ and Mary, the Masters of the earth.

Our purpose, through verses of the Bible, the sciences, and the tools, is to place the Creator's ring on the restored son's finger. We are returning to God in a humbler state than when we left, but all shall be restored to us in greater measure than when we left. There will be much rejoicing by God and his angels over one sinner that repents. Repentance is turning away and going forward. When we come to the great Return, finished with dabbling in the lower nature, to achieving the higher nature, we shall have no fear, and shall have the ability to exercise our authority as sons and daughters of God.

FEAST

All those who would enter the realm of God have been universally invited to a great feast. The universal call has gone out to all and whoever will, may come. We are working toward this goal, for all of us are here to prepare for this great feast.

In Matthew 22:2, we read of a rich man who prepared a great wedding feast for his son. He sent his servants to tell the guests to come, for everything was prepared. The wedding guests made light of this and treated the servants disrespectfully, abusing them greatly. In this age, there is a great desire for truth and revelation among people, but when ministers and servants go into the world serving God, they are abused and mistreated.

It is a privilege for all of us to be invited to the great wedding feast. Yet how many of us are listening to the call? The judgment recorded in Matthew 22 was promised to this world by Jesus if we do not heed the call to the wedding feast. Jesus tells us that the king sent his armies and destroyed those unworthy murderers and burned their cities. The king pronounced them unworthy and went seeking out people in the highways and byways. He gathered both the good and the bad and allowed them to participate in the great event.

The past generation, the old age, is like those who mistreated the servants of God. The judgment of fire will destroy the old creation, and those abiding under the old order will be destroyed by the fire of God's judgment. And those pronounced unholy and unrighteous by the old order will find themselves seated at the Master's table.

For we are living in the day when the Word of God is becoming physically manifested. There will be no more allegories, no more stories, and a definite end to fiction. All

181

will be reality. Even in the New Age, there will be those who will try to enter the wedding without the wedding garment. They will be cast out, and there will be weeping and wailing, and gnashing of teeth. The modern-day wedding garment is simply the glorious light of Christ, the physical manifestation of energy and force in both spiritual and physical action. Without our wedding garment of light, we are doomed. This light of Christ comes to us through the grace of God.

This is an age of spiritual enlightenment. We must abide in this light, for in the true creation of the Creator, all is light, and in it there is no darkness at all. Now, millions and millions of people will enter through the light of Christ. It will be surprising to many of us who we will find sitting at the Master's table. In order to find this light of Christ and be accepted at this wedding feast, we have to deny ourselves, take up our cross, and follow Him, as stated in Luke 14:27.

In Revelation 19:7-9, the story is repeated. This time it is called the marriage of the Lamb. In the New Age, the Lamb of God is the mind. This is a joining of the mind to the Spirit and the physical so that they may perform one function, the glorification of God together. This marriage feast of the Lamb must take place in everyone's being before it can be taken in a universal, literal sense.

"Let us be glad and rejoice and give honor to him, for the marriage of the Lamb has come and his wife has made herself ready...and he said to me, right blessed are they which are called to the marriage supper of the Lamb."

The Spirit has made itself ready for the proper functioning of the light, and all have been invited to participate. Only those with the light of Christ will be accepted. John, the revelator, is testifying to the truth about the marriage feast of the Lamb.

In Matthew 25:10 we read the story of the bridegroom coming and shutting the door. **"The five foolish virgins said: 'Lord, Lord, open to us,' and the answer came, 'Verily, I say to you, I know you not.' Watch therefore, for you know not, neither the day nor the hour, wherein the Son of God comes."**

The Son of God is the center of the marriage, the master of the feast. Through the light of Christ, He created the possibility of our participation in this great event. The Lamb of God must be wedded to the Spirit. After the wedding takes place through the light of Christ, the power of the Creator, our mind and God's mind become one, as it was in the beginning of creation.

Duality ceases to exist at this point for us. Our minds become spiritually perfect and we assume our responsibility as sons and daughters of God. After this has taken place, the world will be under the dominion of the new order and God's plan will have come to pass.

At this great feast, there will be no spot or blemish, no defilement of any kind. The day of the Lord will be accomplished. All will eventually turn toward God. Every knee shall bow and every tongue confess that He is the Christ. Those who have been faithful over a few things will be made rulers of much. Since we are living in a day of active reality, we cannot waste time nor suppose anything. Things actually are or they are not. Our God is a living, vital force, causing all things to be. God's feast is a feast of action and reality, a vital feast and one that all of us must eventually attend.

"Father, be with the ministers of your table, who serve your children the feast of the flesh and blood of Jesus Christ, that all may become, not merely like God, but actually part of his living body, here and now.

Let us not fatten up your congregation with misguided complacency, self-indulgence or pseudo-spiritual food. Let us give them the true nourishment that works toward wholeness and perfection, that they may better perform God's mission, in vigor and strength."

Jesus said to Peter, **"Feed my sheep."** He did not mean feed their self-satisfaction as church-goers with the spiritual candy of flattery, neither to get them so bogged down with their own self-importance that they would become valueless as Christ's servants. Let us rather give them the real nourishment of truth and feed their hunger with holiness and the seed of health, curing their indifference with the vitality of their involvement in Christ. Let them be nourished with his love, his grace, and his Word.

It is true, new students are a little like children, who have to come to the table every time, and to partake under discipline. But let their servant, priest or teacher at the table make sure the food served is not mere warmed-over scraps, neither all sizzling with spice. But let them serve healthful food that will bring them wholeness, giving them balance. Do you ministers stuff your congregations with the pastries and platitudes and hors d'hoeuvres of intellectuality? These are all right for embellishing the meal. But God's truth is the real protein, and God's instructions the vegetables that are always for our benefit.

If we follow these things, the fruits of attainment cannot be far off, for all sustained and faithful effort must be rewarded. One who endures to the end shall inherit a crown.

Do we admonish congregations because it is expected of a minister, with great flourishes of dramatic speech, while secretly chuckling with delight at the great show we are putting on for their benefit – playing the "heavy?" After the sermon is over, they'll shake your hand and compliment you

184

on a great speech – but do they really change? Or have they witnessed a good show, broken up the weekly routine?

Or still worse, do we hurl fire and brimstone at them, threatening them with fear and damnation, to the point of driving them forth from what should have been God's house, into the street, without even the assurance of a loving God? The only alternative to hell offered in cases like this is for people to go and align themselves with the hell and damnation shouters, a fate that hardly seems the lesser of two evils. Most would rather take their chance on living now and to gamble that the day of accounting at the end of the road is distant enough that by the time they arrive there, they'll have figured out an answer, or a way out.

There is a way out without the gamble, which is up to us to teach. We don't have to condemn anyone or join those who do. We can live and follow Christ, become one with Him and live as He lived – loving, giving and doing. His joy was full in God. He knew God loved Him and He loved in return. He loved us. His sharp speech at times was for those who taunted and tried to trap Him and would not listen to the truth.

FIRE

Without the existence of fire there would be no material composition in the universe. The violent chemical reaction that attends the combustion of fuel with oxygen causes heat, which is due to the increased agitation of atoms. In the beginning of creation, vibration emanating from the divine source generated heat before things manifested in material form. Fire has a high rate of vibration, usually experienced as heat. When a piece of wood burns, it will eliminate all impurities and leave a mostly pure product, charcoal. This can be used as a cleansing agent for the body, for water purification and as a base for medicines. We cannot produce fire without the presence of combustible materials. We have to increase the rate of vibration, and then we observe with our five objective senses the manifestation of heat or fire. There is a little heat in everything that exists, though it may be imperceptible to the senses. What is heat? Heat is a form of energy, manifesting to the objective senses as a sensation of hot or cold.

What happens when you light a match and light the wick of a candle? The candle starts to burn continuously and the wax around it begins to disappear. You might think that the wax is what is burning, but then why is the wick necessary? Why will the candle cease to burn if you put a glass over it and make it airtight? Why does air have to mix with the oil or gas in a lamp? Something more than the gas, the oil, or the wick is burning. There is something invisible going on. Half of the laws of nature are being illustrated in this simple example.

Think of how fire changes the nature of something. When the match is burned, what have you got left? Science states that nothing is ever completely or even partially destroyed. There is no more matter in the universe than there was at the beginning of time regardless of what changes or catastrophes have occurred. Fire may consume but it does not destroy. You have consumed the match but you have not destroyed the matter of which it was composed. What makes a match? Not the wood, chemicals or sulphur alone. The piece of wood without the chemicals at the end would just be a toothpick. On the other hand, the chemicals alone without wood would not constitute a match. When fire burns a match, you have not destroyed any of the things that composed it, but the piece of wood is now a piece of charcoal. The chemical elements have changed their nature passing off into a gas of invisible fumes that you can no longer see. The flame was the fire. The flame manifested the chemical changes that were taking place in the wood and in the chemicals at the end of the wood.

Ancient people worshipped fire as a universal deity whose perfect and unadulterated reflection is Heaven. Fire is a substance in God's being and has the function of quickening life or bringing dissolution at death. The alchemists used fire as the material means for purging, purifying, cleansing and regenerating minerals, metals, or elements. The Sun generates the entire supply of heat and energy for the earth and all the planets. Primitive people kept a fire continuously burning in a central place in the village. Today many churches and temples have an eternal flame burning symbolic of an internal reality. The vestal virgins used to attend this flame so that it would never go out. There was a material reason as well as a spiritual reason for keeping the fire burning: so people could light their own hearths. Later the hearth became a sacred place for people to gather. In fact, in some cultures, if a person was an enemy and was able to enter somebody's house and go to the hearth where the fire was burning, they could be given sanctuary. No one would touch them as long as they were there.

When a village fire was put out or accidentally went out, runners were sent to another village to carry the burning embers to rekindle the village fire. On our altars we keep an eternal flame burning to symbolize and acknowledge the one

Spirit of God. We do it to remind ourselves that we are attempting to keep a perpetual light burning within our own beings. Those who have gone through the illumination, and within whom the light has been established, are seeking to maintain a perpetual consciousness of the light of Christ within.

Fire is used on most altars, no matter the religion, and the flame is usually lit with considerable ceremony or ritual. Leviticus 1:7, **"And the sons of Aaron the priest shall put fire upon the altar and lay the wood in order upon the fire."** Throughout Judaism we find many references to the "ever-burning fire," symbolizing God's continuous presence. Even the use of incense in the ancient temples originated through the desire to have some small fire burning that could be easily handled and controlled. Later on, the mystics found that by using certain kinds of incense, a certain rate of vibration would be generated in the air and this would have an effect on the vibratory condition of the room or temple.

In Hebrews 10:27 and 12:29 God is called a "consuming fire." In some high ceremonies and Christian rituals, fire was used as the symbol of the presence of God. In Revelation 1:14, you will find that the risen Lord's eyes were "...as a flame of fire." Most religious worship includes some kind of fire. Fire is a universal symbol, representing the spiritual essence. As fire is everywhere, so God is everywhere. Fire dissolves and dissipates all things causing them to become invisible. Fire was God's shadow. All visible manifestations of God are like a shadow compared to the authentic shining being of God, which is much purer and brighter. We see fire as mystical, celestial and divine in nature, and not merely as material.

The truly illuminated mystic is one who becomes aware of profound wisdom as a result of inner discovery through meditation or revelation. Outward discoveries are seldom as important as those received from within. Real revelation has to do with the spiritual Self within the body, and comes from cosmic sources. Fire was seen in its spiritual, mystical sense as a purging, purifying and regenerating principle. Through the heat of the flames came a newer and higher form of manifestation. In order that we may experience the regeneration, we must be purged of the dross or negation that keeps us from becoming purified and reaching perfection. All of our worldly experiences, trials and tribulations, represent the fire of purification. As we accept the training and discipline of our teacher, our consciousness is raised and a fire drives out the limitations of our thinking and our negative emotional reactions. All of our burning desire and feverish anxiety can raise us to a higher state constituting the fire of regeneration. As our minds and hearts are purified, our body becomes purified. This is why fire eventually symbolized the stage of purgatory. Purgatory purifies our sinful existence preparing us for admission into heaven. Purgatory is really the love a soul has after having tasted the presence of God, and desiring it fully, and then seeks to undergo a purging trial to rid them of anything that might get in the way of a complete ecstatic embrace of oneness with God. Heaven and hell are allegorical states of consciousness, considered by most religions as a literal place. Heaven is where God is, and hell is where God is not. God cannot be where we have closed God out of our hearts, minds and consciousness. Heaven and hell are spiritual and mental conditions of feeling the joy and peace of being in the presence of God or remorse within the soul for having created distance from God. The remorse actually purifies our bodies and minds. St. Paul says that the fires of hell are designed to try the works of human beings, and that the fire of purgatory is to try their persons.

The fire of hell and purgatory are the torment of your mind, the crying aloud of your conscience, the torture of your soul's conviction or the self-condemnation for your sinful acts. The voice of God within you acts as the voice of conscience and chastises you when you do wrong. The fire of God from the heavens consumes your sin, purifies your soul, purges your mind and feelings, and refines your nature. Such flames of purgatory and fires of hell are experienced here and now, sometimes daily and hourly. They are also experienced when we leave our bodies and are more fully aware of not being in the presence of the great love, due to separation we created. The absence of the love burns within us, and the remorse for not having created a relationship with that love, and now we experience the pain of its absence.

We should realize that we cannot go through life in sin and error, committing unjust acts, and remain free from the burning, consuming flames of the fires of hell until we reach a state beyond this life. None of us are free from this fire, and we must suffer it in some way even before we pass beyond. This is a true mystical point of view, completely consistent with what the Master Jesus taught. We must bear in mind that Jesus reminded his disciples of this and told them that the realm of Heaven is within. We add to this that the fires of hell and the tortures of purgatory are ever present in this life, at every turn, and are the ultimate conclusion of every wrong act, every sinful commission or omission, and of every evil thought. Then there is the spiritual condition after we leave our bodies where the fire of God works on us to purge us of any inclinations to evil and to acts which separate us from the love of God.

SYMBOLISM I

These teachings conform to the teachings of the basic world religions and contain the essence and spirit of all ancient teachings, including those of the Holy Bible, the Kabbalah and the Bhagavad-Gita. At the core of all the ancient teachings lie the few, simple laws that the great Creator used when creating the universe. The law of God works on the spiritual plane as well as our material world. The same principles hold true in the life of the soul as in the business world. This makes these teachings different from anything you have studied before. They are definitely not a dogmatic set of instructions.

If God, the great creative power, is the basic substance of the universe, and all things are one, then matter and spirit are one, except that matter is denser than spirit. Our conscious control over these spiritual and material substances makes this a living science. It gives us dominion over the living, moving pulsating process of life. This dynamic force of creation responds to our decision and our wish, and at the same time gives love and life to our sisters and brothers. Spirit and matter are one. Matter is more dense spirit and spirit is less dense matter. We are interested in symbolism because it represents the language of creation in this solar system. It is the language of the way in which the love and power of all things work. It is the language of the basic patterns in the universe that bring spiritual and material supply to us in our everyday life.

Symbolism displays a picture of how we have thought - our concepts of the Creator, how the law of creation works, and how we work with the law. There is only one set of laws that will work through most any form or ritual as long as they are not violated. For example, the law of cause and effect cannot be set aside. Symbolism is also a picture story of the events of history, meaning the things that we as a species have learned to be true. In this way, we do not have to start over again, but

193

can start where others have left off. We can begin each incarnation at the stage of development and progress of the world where others left off, thereby gaining time by their experiences.

Symbolism is a language of signs, like those of mathematics or chemistry. Symbols depict action and how the law works through a certain pattern, bringing the creative energy, God, into the dense world. Most people are only interested in their own personal self and not so much in the world or solar system in which we live and move. We start from our point of reference, what we know as life. In a way, we start in mid-air, because we may not know anything of the heaven world. We do not understand ourselves. We may have had no solid foundation for the working out of our lives. We might have no plan for our future, either on earth and afterward when we pass through the gates of death.

We should be able to start with the knowing of others who have gone before us. We then could take the ball of evolution from them and their experiences and go on with the development of our own inner beings. It is not a case of developing ourselves, as much as it is remembering what we already know within and progressing from there.

Let us take the circle with its center point: The symbol of the circle is one of the oldest and most universal symbols known. It has been used for at least 12,000 years – always interpreted to relate to the center of power, or God. No matter how primitive or advanced we were, we acknowledged the one source of supply in all things - life, creation, power and light. It represents the Godhead, the Creator, the Sun. So we learn a lesson from those who went before. It is a symbol of the Self.

The circle with the center point has represented many things throughout our progress: God with the central creative center, the atom; the cell, or human cell; RA, the Sun God worshipped by the Egyptians, Solar System, the completed cycle of action, the unity of all, God and human beings, that is, the undividedness of this universe, the Earth, the shape of the body itself, the top part of Venus in Astrology, the Zodiac, the Sun, with mind as the center, the wheel and hub, or vortex, and the three circles as the three parts of human beings.

There are only three forms in the whole universe. They are the Circle, the Triangle, and the Square. These forms may be enlarged or made small. They may move in one dimension and not in another. But always, there are just three forms, or portions of them. All things in the physical world are made up of these three patterns so that matter may fill them. There is a law by which we may control matter and what comes into our lives.

Before anything can exist on the earth plane it must first exist in the mind of God. Here we have the world of Archetypes, the world of the thought forms. The world of concrete thought relates to things in the physical world of dense matter. Light is what we see by or what radiates from any object. Some wavelengths are visible to the naked eye. There are also parts of this light that we cannot see. In fact, we see only 1/80th of the actual light existing in the material world. Nevertheless, it still exists and has considerable effect on our everyday life.

The world of thought is like this. It is there, but we do not see it. Yet the law of creation proves its existence. It is from the realm of mind and thought that we obtain our physical body, where the spirit and chemical body meet. This is not an abstract idea or a useless discussion, but a tying together of the mystery of real prayer as the Master Jesus taught it. What could be more essential?

Everything in God's world and in nature, functions through a few definite laws. These laws are just like 2+2=4, or any other rule in mathematics, chemistry or engineering. The law that was spoken of by many of the great Masters, especially Jesus, is the law that gives us choice. Jesus said, **"Your Word shall not return to you void."** Let's take the triangle as taught in the original teachings of the Christian Church. The basic Law of the triangle is the Trinity of Father, Son/Sun and Holy Spirit. At the time it was not taught so that it would be useful, but we need to realize that it works through many forms of matter.

FATHER

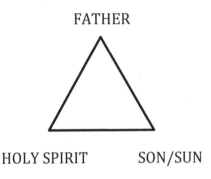

HOLY SPIRIT   SON/SUN

The light energy in the world is the basis of all substance. It is the life force of the Creator flowing through the Sun/Son. It is the eternal triangle, the Law - the visible light that we see with our physical eyes manifesting as color. It is also the invisible light that we do not see with our physical eyes, but which we can see with our spiritual sight. From all the kinds of visible and invisible light, comes the stuff of which dense matter is formed.

An important symbolic language has to do with projection. Projection is the process of seeing important or painful characteristics in other people that we don't recognize in ourselves. For example, we notice in another person how irritating they seem to us. The person has a tendency to be difficult or angry all the time. A tell-tale sign that we are projecting onto someone else some characteristic that we have is that we are very upset or reactive to the other person for having this trait of character. This means that we cannot see that we have this trait because we can only see it in another person. The same is true if we feel someone has qualities that we lack or virtues that we want. We may find ourselves wishing we were like this other person or we will make attempts to get this person to take care of us by representing that virtue or quality for us.

We project onto others those qualities that we lack or those that we hate about ourselves. We make someone else carry those traits as we long to be like another person or secretly hate them for having things we perceive we don't have. Projection is a subconscious language that looks for someone else to carry for us, unlived and unconscious aspects of ourselves. This is the reason relationships become such an important avenue for learning and personal growth. The other person is able to help us see how we expect the friend or partner to personify things that we need to express for ourselves.

In the world of dreams, these projections manifest in the form of same-gender characters, who are within ten years of our biological age. These same-sexed characters personify in our dreams those things that we admire in others or hate in others, depending on whether we feel better than or less than the characters that are symbolic of in our dreams. These projections are shadow characters in our dreams, which means, they are slightly out of our conscious awareness in waking life. They are played out dramatically in our dreams so that we can learn to integrate those projected, cut-off parts of our nature. As we resolve the discrepancy between our waking consciousness and what the shadow parts personify, we can come to wholeness. We will stop projecting our weaknesses or strengths on everyone we meet.

Also in our dreams, we have opposite gender figures that represent the contra-sexual or complimentary parts of our nature. The masculine counterpart in women, and the feminine counterpart in men, presents themselves in dreams to show us the part of us that is less developed and more connected to who we really are. For women, the masculine side is less developed typically and so when the woman is ready, she will experience some interaction and relatedness themes coming up in her dreams when she is starting to develop her masculine energy. So too, men will have dreams of women about their same age, who will represent their feminine side, helping them to get in touch with their feelings and ability to be in a feeling relationship with what is important to them. As a man or woman becomes more integrated with their inside nature and outside expression, their dreams will show the development of the contra-sexual side. They will be moving towards wholeness and balance within themselves and will not be so needy for someone outside them to fix them, heal them, make them happy or take care of things for them.

There are instinctual energies in dreams represented by animals, elements and insects. These are energies that have not as yet become human or accessible, but are still in the instinctual stages of the psyche. As we grow, these energies become more humanized and accessible to our conscious decision. Many of the symbols that arise in our dreams are situation and person related. You cannot know what the dream means unless you know the dreamer somewhat and where the dreamer is developmentally, emotionally and socially. Dream symbols are not fixed and so the books of dream symbols are not that helpful. For example, the symbol of a lake, an ocean or a pond is a body of water. Bodies of water can be ominous, dark, clear, bright, warm or cold. Bodies of water can be many things in the dream. Sometimes they are the divine feminine, the spiritual life, the waters of the subconscious, the divine mother or the unknown. In each

198

case, we would have to know the dreamer to understand the symbolic language of the dreams. Then there is the child archetype, the wise man or woman, mountains and snakes and many other symbols that mean different things with differing situations and people.

We dream approximately five times a night, every forty-five minutes or so in what is REM, the rapid eye movement phase of sleep. The dreams will be shorter in the beginning of the night and gradually get longer and longer towards morning. We have to dream in order to be balanced human beings. The dream is created by the soul and cannot be interfered with by the conscious mind. It is innocent of any outside influence. The dream is a book that has to be read and deciphered and interpreted because of its symbolic language. Everything is important because of the infinite palette of colors and possible images that the dream maker can create. We can remember our dreams if we tell ourselves we want to. Vitamin B6 (25 – 50mg) seems to aid dream memory.

There are three kinds of dreams: objective dreams, compensatory dreams and state-of-the-union dreams. Objective dreams are when we dream of mastering our job when we just got hired for a new job and are trying very hard to figure out how to be good at it. Compensatory dreams are when you dream that you are super competent or wonderful in the dream, which is a way for the psyche to bring you up to balance from feeling bad about yourself. Or you can dream you are unprepared for an exam, naked in a presentation, or otherwise not doing so well, as a way for the psyche to bring down your sense of self-importance to balance you out. The state-of-the-union dreams are telling the dreamer in symbolic language how things are going in life. They are the hardest to interpret because they seem like you know what it is saying but you really need help understanding their meaning. There are two questions to ask to help you understand your own dreams: 1. How do I feel inside the dream while this scene is going on? And 2. What is wrong with this picture? What makes no sense in these images? It is important not to try to think about the dream outside the dream looking in. Stay in the dream so you know how you felt in the dream.

An example: a woman dreamt that her nine month old new baby was starving and dying in the corner of a room. She thought someone else was taking care of her, but when she looked, it was almost dead. She woke up crying and really scared and worried. This means that nine month plus nine months ago, so eighteen months ago, she conceived of some new endeavor, new path, new relationship, new job, new home, new something that she is being told by the dream she has been neglecting and allowing to die within her. She may be losing interest in what was conceived eighteen months ago or she is being warned to really take it on to revive and feed it and juice it with life and energy. She needs to be very serious about what she wants or that baby, that new endeavor, will die.

SYMBOLISM II

We have been able to see and know that all things that manifest have two different polarities. Like the poles of a magnet, there is a positive and a negative pole. The triangle describes the action of all the formulas of energy, whether electrical, chemical or mechanical. The triangle is the basis of life in action, and is demonstrated by its movement of itself about the central point: God. Energy is the great creative power.

It does not make any difference whether we are using the term God, Allah, Yahweh, Jehovah or Brahma, because they are all one and the same. They represent the same basic power we refer to as "God." We are talking about how God creates and supports all of creation.

The square represents the four elements of material manifestation. Here we see the opposites working together. Fire and air are the working elements of combustion. Water and earth are the components of solids in creation. Our body is also made up of these elements. Water and earth form the negative pole of earth life. Fire and air form the positive pole, or spiritual part, of earth life.

In our physical body, our personal universe, the earth furnishes us with minerals and denser material. Water makes up more than 90% of our brain and 70% of our physical body. Water attracts the psychic and spiritual forces. Thus, we have the attraction of the spiritual body to the denser matter of the material body. Air conveys the life force, or Christ force, into the lungs. This is picked up by the blood. When a great deal of dross or toxins accumulate in a body, a disease may manifest. Then the fire element creates a fever to burn out the disease. This action strikes a balance and we may once again have good health.

There are three Master Forms: Circle, Triangle and Square. All designs, machines, buildings, physical bodies, and things of nature use these same forms in some variation. The circle or sphere is a universal form and is the basic building block in the solar system. In the whole universe, there are only three forms: the circle, the triangle and the square. All things in this physical world are made of these three patterns. The pattern, of course, is first formed in the mind of God. Then, through the law, it comes into the physical world.

Step 1: We first must become conscious of God, the great creative power, the circle. Therefore, we may realize that God is a part of every cell in our body.

Step 2: The triangle represents the three steps of the law, the process of creation. In this we begin to know the power of the Word left to us by the Master Jesus from God. This power existed from the beginning, but was re-taught by the Master Jesus and our Mother Mary. Through this triangle we have the power of choice as to what is going to come into our world.

Step 3: Here we form a pattern and then let go of it, knowing that it will work and accept that it is accomplished. Then the elements of the square will filter down into the dense world, coming into manifestation. Thus we can create any and all things.

Symbolism is a means of understanding and using the universal language of God. A symbol does not represent one word, as we use words, in English, French or German. It is a sign that is all-encompassing, that conveys a picture of a thing, or a force, and the feeling about it.

Regardless of your religion, we are more interested in teaching you what you have not been taught about your faith, than trying to suggest that what you were taught was wrong. We are dedicated to enabling you to be free to manifest God and mind in peace and happiness without fearing anything. You alone can manage your own life. You do this by knowing the universe you live in, by knowing the tools you have to work with, and by knowing yourself and your neighbor.

The discovery of Fire was the breakthrough in consciousness for people. Out of this evolved the teachings of the Word and the eternal flame. These teachings have a divine substance and a spiritual basis. If you could see this fire in the atmosphere around you, you could see where the life force comes from. You would find that there were billions upon billions of sparks of life force of the Word spoken by God. And even the strong word, which denotes divine authority, puts it into a simple form. This is the 'fiat,' the divine Word within us. These tiny life sparks are a living material reality of the Word of life. The Word is the fiat of the life, or the eternal flame kept burning in the mind of God. In most temples and churches in the world, you will find an eternal flame burning as a reminder that we are dependent on the creative Word of our wondrous and nameless Creator.

This is why we have the First Commandment - for from God flows light, life and love through the great Christos, the first-born Son of God.

COMMUNICATION I

Communication is the movement of God's energy flowing from the Creator to the creation in the form of light, life and love. Communication is all the ways the love of God is distributed to all parts of creation, especially to human beings. Communication is the connecting link between past life experiences and the life we are now living. The dictionary defines 'communication' as "the act of passing along information, transfer by talking, writing letters, messages, means of going from one place to the other, and connection."

In order for the state of thinking and feeling called brother-sisterhood to become a reality, it is necessary that all communication be clear. When we have a universal picture that embraces life in all forms throughout this solar system, then communication can be clear. We must understand how others worship and understand that all religions and philosophies are similar, except in what each denomination has left out of their teachings.

We brought you the understanding of symbolism, so that as you go about your daily duties in the world, you may observe the way light, life and love move and manifest through experienced observation. By studying the material forms such as buildings, art, fashions, nature or one of God's beautiful flowers, we can observe the circle, the triangle and square in all forms of creation. The architecture of a church and its interior, or the symbolism of a ritual or a religious service, is also an expression of the way God touches creation and human beings. All of these are communications between God and people.

Rituals build a visible realization of the Creator's laws of this universe, and thereby build up the feeling that gives us the ability to work with the law of Creation. When we attend a church service, we can be conscious of this force in action.

Most religious services have a uniform and common pattern of prayer and worship that tells a very similar story. How spiritually developed we are determines whether we are expressing the teachings of the outer or inner temple. Let us define "outer and inner temple." In most ancient religions there were three classes of people who attended the temple service. First, the multitude was allowed only to approach the temple to worship and bring burnt offerings. They never came beyond the brazen altar of sacrifice. Second level was the student priests and disciples who were admitted to the service of God in the temple and came as far as the second veil or court of the temple. Third – only the High Priest was admitted behind the second veil or curtain into the center where the Shekinah of the Ark of the Covenant was placed.

In the Mystery Schools, we would find the three qualifications as:

First: Students who have awakened to their spiritual responsibility and are striving to reach the higher life of lighted beings by study and practice.

Second: The initiate who has taken a certain obligation to themselves, whereby they agree to love, honor, and obey the Inner Self, and dedicate themselves to a life of service to humankind as a means of approaching the inner court, and attaining the conscious Realization of the God within.

Third: The Priest - the Mystic - one who has persisted and shown their devotion in such a manner that they are now involved in the deeper spiritual work. They are being prepared to safely pass behind the veil, and when they were ready, the teacher brings them into Self-Realization.

In the New Age, the age we entered in the year 1883, the first court or veil was dissolved. In other words, at this time, the outer and second court of the temple joined and became one.

The outer court is where the masses of people must now adapt themselves. This leaves but one inner court, which is that of the higher evolvement. In modern times, those entering this court are the ones who devote their lives to the service of God and to their fellow beings. We are now obliged to love, honor, and obey the Inner Self in service to our neighbors. We must become conscious of the great creative power within. Whether we have reached this stage of evolution or not, it will soon be a question of whether we are able to handle seen and unseen potencies of the reality of God. Eventually, those who do not choose to love God and other people will no longer be able to live on Earth, because that will be the new level of consciousness required to be here. Those of the inner court, whose development has brought them to a point of consciousness where they have learned to handle the power and tools of mind, sight and hearing, manifest complete freedom on both the seen and unseen planes of existence.

EXERCISE: Observe during your work day the many objects you use, wear, and see that contain the three basic forms of creation.

In this world and between worlds, we have a problem of communication. If there is a problem of communication, it makes it doubly hard to have peace. Because if we do not understand our neighbor, certainly we will not feel safe to relay our thoughts to them, not knowing if they will agree. Certainly we know that without peace within us, it is not possible to have peace between neighbors. Without peace, all science, philosophy, religion and art are a waste of time and effort. Peace within the country will carry over into peace between people, and good communication will follow. Where there is peace, there is no fear. It is always fear of one thing or another that brings about war.

Human beings are composed of many parts. As we speak, think, and have emotions, our minds and bodies are sending out electrical impulses, not only in the form of brain waves, but as electromagnetic impulses. This is also a form of communication, whether we are conscious of it or not. As we use the one mind in thinking, we are sending out dynamic energy waves, which, when picked up by other people (and they are always picked up by others unconsciously), have an effect on their thinking and emotions. People who are generally not conscious, or intentional, in their thoughts and feelings will receive the thoughts and emotions of whatever broadcast they are unwittingly tuned to. This is a form of telepathy.

The mass mind is the most powerful influence on people as a whole. It is made up of the thinking and emotions of all the people in a city or a congested area. These thoughts and emotions give off electrical impulses. The thinking and emotions of the general population, customs and generally accepted ideas, create the atmosphere of a city. People do not have to be affected by this if they are vigilant about keeping their own personal thinking and emotions clear. But in the case of the masses those with the clearest and strongest concepts will produce the most powerful and manifested thought. These thoughts may be positive or negative, and will determine the pattern that affects those people as a whole. So, everyone is creating a pattern of thinking and emotions which determines everyone's living conditions. This is another form of communication.

We have five physical senses - taste, touch, hearing, smell and sight. So likewise, we have another set of five spiritual senses that register things we do not see or hear physically. These are as important as the physical senses. They are our means of expanding beyond time and space. Included in this list of spiritual senses is telepathic communication, which is related to intuition. Our extrasensory functions allow us to communicate with people who have left their bodies at death, or have gone through transition, as we describe it.

These teachings are a part of God's mind, and therefore not confined to any particular church. They are a part of the true science of being and the tools that enable human beings to master their lives. Life is continuous, ever-evolving and ever-changing, for where there is no movement, there is no life. The multiplication of cells and our very physical existence is dependent on spiritual forces that operate the autonomic nervous system of our physical bodies. Therefore, it is absolutely impossible to disregard the spiritual world. If we denounce it, or deny its existence, we cut off its life. Sit quietly with eyes shut and visualize any one part of your body at a time for a few minutes, and open your eyes. Note how different that part feels. Continue this exercise for a week and see, by daily application, the change in your physical vitality.

May God bless you, as you open new doors to wisdom.

COMMUNICATION II

We have discussed many ways in which communication is a natural part of our lives that helps us gain balance, harmony and freedom of movement. Now we are going to talk about another method of communication that involves reaching the great creative force of this solar system. This is really cosmic telepathy. Here we are able to communicate intelligently with the Creator who created this universe. We communicate with God through the Law of the Triangle, in order to control what we are going to accept in our life. Our ability to choose, which was given by God, is our personal application of the law. We can accept what we want in our lives, and our knowledge of how to communicate with the Creator will fulfill what we accept.

Conscious application of our spiritual tools will put us in communication with anyone, whether they are in a physical body or a spiritual body. With this type of power in our consciousness, we are free to travel at will and are no longer confined by the physical body. What most people regard as a miracle is really the working of a definite law and order. Do you really see very much of the physical world? We are uncovering connections for you to transmit messages. The wiring has been there since the beginning of time, but you did not have your instrument properly attuned and did not know how to use it. There is always a way, and if one person can do it, anyone can do it. Anyone can do it, if they will but work at it and work with it. In Psalm 145:16, **"You opened your hand and satisfied the desire of every living thing."**

The Bible is a handbook that has the keys to all the secrets of nature, if we will but stop and think. In Luke 12:31 it is written, **"Seek you first the Kingdom of God, and all these things shall be added to you."**

There is one more way of communicating, called the art of projection. If we wish to see what has happened to a student or friend who is visiting a foreign land or traveling somewhere, and we may have a premonition about them that they might need help. It is a fact that we can sit in our own house and project ourselves, and locate and see the friend we are concerned about. We can give help if needed. It is also possible for us to have the other person see us. Even though they may not be fully developed spiritually, they may feel reassured by our contact.

People become advanced beings through their own spiritual evolution. Such thinking and understanding of life are at a higher level than most people experience. We are not talking about some people having greater divinity than others because we all have the same degree of divinity and all have the same Self from God. But there is something else in such people that make them above average, something that gives them a natural or easy understanding of God and the law and their relation to the Creator. They seem advanced in mental power, in ability to see and understand, to hear and realize, to be intuitive, clairvoyant and clairaudient. These people become successful in life, happy, prosperous, learned and strong. Almost always, some special spiritual training is necessary to help them attain these things. That is why there is a school like ours with its higher teachings, intended to develop and help people express their more noble qualities of being.

We do not close the door to people who think they can achieve the heights of a true follower, for all will learn something and gain some help and advantage, even though it may not manifest until their next incarnation. If the last incarnation ended with high aspirations, noble thinking, and a longing for greater knowledge and greater happiness, with no bitterness toward others, no hatred toward enemies, no sinful desires, injustice, or cruelty; then early in this life, this same high level of attainment or development will have come forward, regardless of the place of our birth, our environment, station in life, wealth, or education. In this sense, we are not all born equal, and because of this fact, our present life is, to a great extent, due to what we made of it in the last incarnation. Of course, those who started early in the last incarnation will constitute the advanced people of this age.

What does it mean to be one of these? It means everything that is heartily discouraging to others. Did you ever stop to think that there is nothing so thankless in this world as devoting yourself to humanitarian work? If we develop ourselves to where the healing gift of body, mind and heart is easy to apply and we quickly and conveniently go about giving personal or absent healing treatments that are almost like miracles, we will find that people seldom feel grateful for the healing work. They may even say, as I have heard them say so many hundreds of times: "Perhaps I was not as sick as I thought I was," or, "Perhaps nature would have cured me anyway." When so little thanks or appreciation is expressed when we are healed, we can easily imagine people having even less appreciation when they are helped with a personal problem. The attitude on the part of the masses seems to be that if anyone has any divine power expressing through them, then it is a gift of God and is no credit to that person. They should not be thanked for their effort, or for the possession of such a gift. It is as though God bestowed these gifts on one without that person applying any effort to be prepared or to be worthy.

The most discouraging thing for spiritually advanced souls is that our whole lives are made up of two experiences: either we are very happy, or very sad. We sense joy as few can sense it, and we get the utmost happiness out of life. Then at times we are sorrowful, sad at heart, and it seems as though the sorrow of the world rests on our shoulders. The Master Jesus typified that condition often. Few will understand you, few will sympathize with you, and that is what makes it so hard; but you must be prepared to meet these challenging conditions. You must be able to meet everyone and anyone, and admit that they are different in nature, different in development, but one in Christ.

As success comes to you in life and you attain the necessary abundance, and great joy seems to be present, you must be able to be alone sometimes. By being alone, you will have to pass through sadness and sympathy for those who have not, those who are in sorrow or pain. You must be ready to share your abundance, for you know that if you do not share it, it may all be taken from you, and when you again desire what is necessary, it will not manifest or will not be forthcoming. You learn the truth of these words: "The things we value the most are the things we have given away." This was referring to material things and beautiful non-material things given to others to make them happy.

A mystic on the spiritual path understands that in all our planning, thinking and building, we must have others in mind. Then we begin to attune ourselves with the universal mind. We then attract, receive, and give. But for this reason, our lives are also discouraging at times, to ourselves and others. We must be willing to see our families do without some luxuries, so that we may give to others who have a greater need of help. We must be willing to face criticism for our actions, which are seldom understood by our friends, and always misinterpreted by our enemies. Even our success in life may bring criticism, for we are envied, and some may say that we have secret powers that are uncanny. We find our greatest trial, however, in living our vows. Well-meaning friends, not knowing the true value of our present association, will recommend other channels for our altruistic activities. We may be tempted to yield, believing that those other channels of service might widen our scope of activities and that we might better help humanity through diversified methods.

At times, our powers and abilities will become so great that we are tempted to feel that as a chosen son or daughter of God, we can go on alone independently. This, as some have learned, is a serious mistake. True adepts, who have reached the heights, never cut themselves off from their brother and sister workers and teachers. They realize that, in a cosmic sense, this displays ingratitude and a lack of true mystical humility. Almost all who have done this have severed the golden thread that has helped to keep them attuned with God. And this is due, not so much to the loss of connections, as to the reason they were severed.

Stop right here and ponder over the words just given. You want to advance to the very highest level of the work. You want to be a true disciple and attain self-mastery and be a power for good, with health and prosperity. Are you willing to face the difficulties, tests and trials mentioned above? If you are, you must express that determination.

We may go through life and accidentally discover here and there some great fundamental truth, and that truth in and of itself may be inspiring. Yet, it is not practical unless it can be related to other truths of the cosmic. When we accidentally discover a truth, we do not know its sequence in the cosmic plan. The Tree of Life gives you these truths in their sequential order. As you receive a new truth each week or each month, you gradually conceive the whole plan. You finally know just exactly where to fit that truth into your life where it will do the most good. This helps us by providing a blueprint of the proper life, one compatible with cosmic law and order. It provides a method of assembling knowledge, presented in a manner that will best serve our needs.

Some become discouraged when they find they must really study. They expected short, easily remembered laws to be given them with no notes, no practicing and no thinking. Students hope and dream that the teacher could just wish some power into their hands, and that would be all there was to it. Others think that merely being initiated is enough. But Jesus said, "Follow me." Our teachings do not interfere with any religion, East or West. They do not interfere, because they contain all the truths, all the laws, and all the principles that make for a religious worship and reverence toward God.

POWER

When we speak about Power we are talking about the unlimited power of human beings. The dictionary defines 'power' as 'physical force or energy.' Power is the capacity to act physically. In electrical engineering, it states that the shorter time it takes to do a piece of work, the more power is manifest. In other words, the shorter the time, the more power is manifest in doing equal work.

Watts is an electrical term for power or current. "I" (current flow) multiplied by "R" (resistance) equals "E"(electro-motive force). The formula is "I" X "R" = "E". ("R" = a percentage) This demonstrates that the laws of science explain the practice of following Jesus' teachings. In other words, if we do not resist the Christ force, the light, life and love will flow through us (energy = light, life, and love). In the law of Prayer when we want things to come into our lives, like a prayer for healing, it will manifest in relationship to the amount of resistance we have to receiving it. The Master Jesus had no resistance to the love and life of God, so a greater current flowed through him, and the fullness of power was manifest. His healings took place right then and there. As He spoke to someone, it took place immediately.

If the current that is flowing meets with little or no resistance, greater power will be manifest through you. I X R = E. ("R" is always a fraction or percent because total absence of resistance would equal total movement of power through you.) The dictionary also defines 'power' as 'authority.' Since our authority is from the source, the Creator, it is possible to use the power of God to manifest all of our desires in life. Power is manifested as light, for light is matter in a less dense form. If matter sheds its mass and travels with the speed of light, we call it radiation or energy. We call this a conversion of form. If the energy congeals and becomes inert, we can see it as mass and then it has become matter.

There is a certain definite amount of energy in the universe. It can be generated and produced from another form of energy by forcing electrons to move in a particular pattern. Remember, the less resistance we have, the more we will generate and demonstrate power. This goes right along with a very old saying, "Let go and let God." If we do not let go, God's power cannot flow through us, and the Christ life, the Spirit, cannot move to do the work and manifest. It takes an awful lot of power to regenerate the physical body and to reorganize it and bring it back to the normal pattern of health. We think that regeneration is just a figure of speech, that we just become stronger, and that nothing else is really happening. This is not true; for regeneration follows a definite path.

If we are seeking illumination and are letting go of the old resistant patterns while learning to take in more light, we will find that a great deal of power manifests in us, and a very definite physical change takes place. Regeneration takes place during periods of initiation and during illumination. From three days to nine months, the regeneration begins to take place beginning with the starting of the light. As the light does the work, it demonstrates its power.

The three basic uses of power are Prayer, Meditation and Blessing. The power of the Word, using God's energy, is an action that demonstrates the use of the life force and the light of Christ in the power of Prayer. The Power of Meditation is demonstrated in the use of the mind and law of God. The Power of Blessing is demonstrated in the use of the Spirit and the Christ light.

In I Chronicles 29:11 we read, **"For Yours, O God, is the greatness and power and glory and the beauty and the majesty and the honor."** This depicts the nature and characteristics of the power of God. In Psalms 62:11 it is written, **"God has said this once; twice have I heard this;**

that power belongs to God." It is of utmost importance that we know and acknowledge that all energy and force originates in the Creator that there is but one basic power or source of energy.

In Matthew 28:18-20 it says, **"And Jesus came up and spoke with them and said to them, 'All power in heaven and on earth has been given to me. Just as my Father has sent me, I am also sending you.'"** Jesus is telling us that when we accept his invitation to serve him, he sends us out into our mission giving us the same power God gave him.

The Sun, the visible manifestation of an invisible center, is the source of all energy. From the sun there radiates into the surrounding space the primary energy of nature. This energy is dual in nature: (+) and (-), male and female. It has the characteristics of a wave and produces a vibratory condition wherever it strikes.

Thermodynamics, the study of energy, has two laws. 1. Energy can neither be created nor destroyed; and 2. Energy may transform from one kind into another. Mechanical energy may change into electrical; spiritual energy may change into material. In changing, energy always changes from a higher form, where it is easily available, to a lower form, where is it less available, from an organized state to a less organized state.

Energy, being an active, positive cause, must obey the law of the Triangle. Energy has the ability to produce a manifestation, have an effect. The active cause (+) must always act upon a suitable, passive recipient, or negative (-) cause. Forces of nature must operate to produce a manifestation. One must be strong and active while the other is a recipient. Yet the two causes must be related to one another and bear a definite affinity or attunement.

Manifestation is a perceptible effect on the material plane observable to the senses, and on the immaterial plane, observable to the spiritual senses. Space is an area of higher vibration with an atmosphere that is less dense. We go up, not in distance, but in vibration. As we do, the density grows less and grows more invisible. Matter represents the stuff or structure of the universe. In every part of nature we observe action and reaction, polarity. Polarity is in light and dark, cold and hot, ebb and flow of the tides, in female and male, in expiration and inspiration of plants, animals and humans, centripetal and centrifugal forces. The material world is dual in nature: spirit and matter, man and woman, subjective and objective, in and out, upper and lower, motion and rest, yes and no.

We seek greater power, a higher life and infinite knowledge so that we might draw closer to God and serve God more effectively in earth. Most of the world feels powerful because we can smash atoms and create nuclear energy. Our sense of control over these forces is minute compared to the power and force contained in the invisible atom. If we connect to the universal power as easily and systematically as we create weapons of war, we would accomplish a great victory. For the power within us is far greater than any force produced by any engine or machine we have ever devised. We experience power moving through our minds. The brain has no power by itself without our consciousness. It is now time for us to learn to use the wondrous forces that God loaned to us. The knowledge of this energy and power makes it possible for us to control and use all the powers of the universe.

We must dedicate ourselves to using everything we learn and power we gain only for good and for helping to bring more light, life and love to our fellow humans and our beloved planet. Our intention is to place in your consciousness the universal truths of creation. With this knowledge, you will be able to understand everyone, including yourself. We must learn about our physical body and the forces of energy and vitality they contain. There are forces in our body that vibrate and can convey energy from one part of our body to another. Certain places in the body have a greater degree of sensitivity and output of energy than others. The energy flows through the principle nerve trunks, the most important being our two hands and two feet. The hands receive and transmit tremendous energy and power if our conscious intention directs it. We can run this power through our fingertips, especially through the thumb and first and second finger. This force can be registered on sensitive instruments, used by magnetic healers. The right hand is more powerful and can be placed at certain locations on the spine to heal certain conditions. When we suffer from pain, we need to become quiet and relaxed as much as we can for a few minutes.

When using the fingertips, do not apply pressure. Pressure means nothing. Place the two fingers and thumb of the right hand firmly to the flesh, and concentrate your mind to that part of the body or organ where pain or difficulty exists. Pain is the body's way to warn you that something is not working well and energy is not moving like it should. Don't try to obliterate pain because it is educational. We seek instead to relieve the condition that is causing the pain. Within about three minutes, the person suffering will begin to feel vibrations, or a tingling sensation, out of their fingertips. At this point, the treatment may cease. Usually, in five or ten minutes, the pain will begin to subside and the condition of the body will go back to normal.

If we are suffering from pain of any kind, we should be relaxed and quiet for a minute or two and locate the pain. For pains in the head, face and neck: apply the fingertips of the right hand to the neck just behind and below the left ear, about the level of the mouth, and below the mastoid bone. For pains in the chest, upper part of the back, and arms: apply the fingers of the right hand to the back of the neck on the left side of the spine. For pains in the abdomen, back sides and hips, apply the fingertips to the left side of the spine between the shoulder blades. For pains in the limbs, feet and groin: apply the fingertips to any point on the left side of the spine between five and ten inches below the collar bone, or the center of the spine.

Because we have sent curative vibrations of electrical energy into the body, we have restored and re-balanced the forces in the spiritual and physical body. We have furnished the energy so that nature can do its own work and perform its cure. Knowing these few things does not make us physicians or healers. In certain situations, we can help our friends and family, but we would have to know quite a lot more to be a spiritual healer. The teachers of this Order have gleaned much information from many great schools and we are giving this to you in conjunction with the teachings of Jesus and Mary. A good Christian should be a good physician. Jesus Christ said the Word of God will deliver to us whatever we ask. Remember that the greatest healings are those of the heart, the mind and the soul. Healings of the body are minor in comparison.

Keep in mind that regardless of how much knowledge we have, a good healer obeys the first commandment, "Love God with all your heart, with all your mind, with all your strength and with all your soul. Then the healing gifts will be given to you.

THE LAW I

We call this the law of God's being, or the law of the universe. The law of God is the blueprint for how all the energies and love of God move within God's being to take care of every part of creation. The law of the Triangle and the law of God are the same thing. Our inherent nature is forever seeking to express itself in terms of freedom. The great love of the Creator insures this freedom through our consciously activating the law.

The law is the wiring that connects every part of creation to the Creator. The law is the network and fabric of love that feeds every part of God, both seen and unseen, with whatever the creation needs. The conscious parts of creation decide what they want. Jesus said, **"It is God's good pleasure to give you the Kingdom."** This means that God wants every part of creation and especially the conscious, creative parts to have everything they need and want, to be able to grow, learn and create. It is through God's law that God makes it possible for all prayers to work for anyone. Anything that we ask for is given to us by God. It is the law of God that responds to our request.

The law must carry out and fulfill the requests and wishes of every human being because it is God's desire to make sure we get what we want. The law is impersonal; it has no conscious choice about what it will respond to because it must accept every request and fulfill it. The law knows what to do so that it makes those prayers happen, but it does not have any choice about whether it likes the request or not. Whatever a human being wants or decides, unleashes the power and love of God to make that take place. The power of your choice and the amount of feeling and conviction you have in requesting from God will influence how fast things happen. Some people make half-hearted requests and doubt themselves in the asking and so the law will be slowed down in its operation. It will still fulfill your request and respond to your desire, but it will be in proportion to the energy you put into it. What you put into it, you get back. That is the law.

You activate the law by use of mind and feelings. If you are merely cerebral in your activation of the law, then the result will be slow. If you put feeling into what you decide to choose, then the law will be swift in its response. Remember it is God's wish to make sure you have what you want. The law has no choice what to respond to. Many people feel that God will only answer requests that make sense or are good things. But God will give every conscious being whatever they choose. That is how human beings learn. They make choices and then have to live them out until they change their minds and hearts and make better decisions.

God is the life at the center, the core, the Self, the infinite love. God is all goodness, peace and love. God is the essence of our being and is love and purity. There is one ultimate reality, one mind, and one power and there is no other energy. The law is the personality of God and the way God expresses. Through the law, we create because we could not create in any other way than the way God set things up. Only ignorance of the truth keeps us from experiencing this great freedom and power of having absolute dominion over our lives through the law. Only the limitations of our consciousness prevent us from experiencing strength, success, vitality, material supply and spiritual revelation.

God is love, so, we are only in bondage to our misconceptions and lack of experience in this Solar System. When we have attained cosmic consciousness, and are able to operate with the Self, we can gradually work to the point where we will not be bound by matter. God's perfect love created the universe. We cannot encompass God, yet we will always be in God and of God. The law is the servant of the eternal God. The limitless power of God gives us the status of co-creator in that our word will be fulfilled.

If we want to learn how to live, we must discover how to create in mind. Thoughts go into this infinite medium and are able to manifest simply by knowing the truth. Karmic law is not fate, but cause and effect. It is a taskmaster to the foolish, and a servant to the wise. Our conscious mind operates within a subconscious field that is creative. Think of the conscious mind as the motivator of the Spirit which activates the law. One is a complement of the other, and we cannot express without a union of both. As a seeker of the path straight up the mountain and not around it, we accept our gifts wherever we find them. God created the Self as the conscious and individualized center of action and expression through us. The divine being can only express through us as our consciousness allows it because God does not force us to do anything. This is the essence of all teaching. God's light, life and love created humans to be instruments to express God, whenever they become willing to be such instruments. The Apostle Paul stated it this way, **"In God we live, and move and have our being."**

The law works for everyone alike. If we are only able to conceive a little of God's goodness, that is as much as we can experience. We must defy the idea of a power of evil in opposition to the power of good. In God there is only goodness and light. The distorted consciousness of angels or humans has created evil which is against God. But God cannot will evil and is not in any battle with evil. Light and good always win. Primitive human beings believed in many gods and powers, but these were merely attributes of the one God. As we progressed we came to believe in one God. Then we became confused and believed that the universe was divided against itself with God on one side and the devil on the other. A realm divided against itself cannot stand. This misconception taught that the devil has power to disturb in equal proportion to God's ability to bless. It also taught that souls can be damned and God can be vengeful and hateful. The Creator knows no evil. God made human beings in God's own image and spiritual likeness. We were made perfect and have an endless existence in God. This is why we are called part of the body of God. God holds us in mind visualizing our perfection, since the divine mind is not able to conceive of an imperfect idea. Since we are part of God, we must be inherently perfect, being part of the divine being. Yet we imagine ourselves to be alone and separate, and we become sick and we suffer. That is because we are individuals and can do what we want. Ecclesiastes 7:29 **"God has made us upright, but we have sought out many inventions."** We may deface or even destroy ourselves, but we cannot destroy the divine image within us.

By baptism we are saved through the bath and fire of the Holy Spirit, or the projection of the personality of God, which regenerates and renews us. Baptism actually resurrects the reality of the spiritual body in us. Jesus overcame the separation from God by accepting the universal realization. St. Augustine said, "Let us rejoice and give thanks that we have become not only Christians, but Christ." Sisters and brothers, do you understand the grace of God, our Father? Let us stand in admiration. Rejoice. We too can become Christed and part of the Holy Family.

Psalm 145:16 **"You opened your hand and satisfied the desire of every living thing."**

Jesus taught the truth of the process of life and meant every word. Remember the statement, "As we think, so we are." This is true, as well. Jesus said, **"Your word shall not return to you void."**

THE LAW II

God created the universe and all life consistent with the law of God's being. That law states that what is sown will be reaped; that every action generates an equal reaction; that we receive what we ask for through our words, thoughts, emotions and actions. God created the universe this way because it works. And God created all conscious beings to live within this law so that they can come to understand how to be conscious co-creators of their lives and their experiences. We do this through experiencing the results of our actions. God also wants us to be absolutely free to decide for ourselves how we want to live. We can therefore choose anything we want to have in our lives if we know how to clearly create it within the universal mind of God.

Through an increase in our consciousness and our understanding of the use of the law, we can affect how our lives unfold. We were given the Ten Commandments and then we need to see the results of our actions. We can determine how to live our lives in order to reap the results from what we desire and do.

Except when there is a karmic condition, or a reason God has for our having a physical dysfunction, health and sickness are largely manifestations of what we are thinking and feeling. Physicians generally agree that over 70% of our illnesses are caused by our mental and emotional states and health habits. In conditions of intense anger, the blood will leave chemical deposits in the joints of the body which can limit movements. Negative emotions, in most cases, are the cause of immense physical suffering. A healthy mind generally reflects itself in a healthy body. This shows that we are relaxed and the energy and power of God are flowing through us because they flow wherever there is no resistance to them.

The following is a list of some physical problems and the thinking or emotional patterns that may bring them about. Each disease may result from only one cause or several causes in combination.

HEADACHE: Resentment or resistance. Confusion; worry; anxiety; tension; suppressed emotions; self-criticism; invalidating the self. The opposite of Peace.

LUNG TROUBLE: A consuming passion; an unexpressed emotion; a strong desire; depression; grief; fear of taking in life; not feeling worthy of living life fully.

EYE TROUBLE: Not liking what you see in your own life or in your family. Belief in limited or separated vision; thoughts of dishonesty; suspicion; fear; desolation; unhappiness.

CONSTIPATION: Refusal to release old ideas; stuck in the past; stinginess; belief in limitation, burden, bondage and fear.

HEART TROUBLE: Sudden shock; terrific loss (particularly loss of love); fear; thoughts of strain and disharmony; disappointment in or by a loved one; financial reversals; lack of joy; hardening of the heart.

PARALYSIS: Thoughts of restriction; fear; terror; resistance; escaping a situation or person.

ASTHMA, HAY FEVER: Thoughts of anxiety, strain, indecision, deep-seated worry; feeling stifled; fear of life; suppressed crying.

BLOOD PROBLEMS: Lack of consciousness of love; a break in the rhythmic harmony of life; lack of joy; lack of the circulation of ideas;(hardening of arteries) fear of growing old.

NERVOUSNESS: fear, anxiety, struggle, rushing; not trusting the process of life; strain; disharmony; worry; remorse over past actions; fear of the future.

FEVERS: Fear and discord; anger; burning up.

INSANITY: Fleeing from the family; escapism; withdrawal; violent separation from family; delusion that one has lost Self-consciousness, loss of belief in One Mind. God's mind is perfect.

FEET TROUBLE, LEG TROUBLE: Fear of the future; not willing to move; unwillingness to be guided into all Truth, to be led by the ever-present Mind.

HAND TROUBLE, ARM TROUBLE: Unwillingness to grasp Divine ideas, to grasp Reality; or unwillingness to let go of what one should let go of.

FALSE GROWTHS, CANCERS AND TUMORS: Destructive emotions, desires, or ideas; depression; misunderstanding; maladjustment; frustration; nursing old hurts and shocks.

OBESITY: Gluttony, caused by unexpressed longings and fear of food; fear; need for protection; running away from feelings; insecurity; self-rejection; seeking fulfillment.

KIDNEY, LIVER, BLADDER TROUBLE: Worry; anxiety; fear; criticism; sudden shock and grief (kidneys); mental irritation: anger (bladder); memory of unpleasant experiences; hard and tense thoughts (liver); thoughts of greed, selfishness and jealousy (all three organs).

STOMACH, BOWEL TROUBLE: Worry; distrust; anxiety; hurt feelings; discouragement; disappointment; inability to assimilate the new; super-sensitiveness.

INSOMNIA: Sometimes shock; grief or anxiety; fear; not trusting the process of life; guilt; often the inability to let go of the affairs of the day - opposite of Perfect Trust in God.

RHEUMATISM: Thoughts of fear and bondage; feeling victimized; lack of love; chronic bitterness; resentment.

INDIGESTION: Condemnation of food; overeating and eating the wrong foods; gut level fear, dread, anxiety (Although most foods will be acceptable for anybody who recognizes that food is a spiritual idea or substance).

COLDS, FLU, INFLUENZA: Confusion; fear; susceptibility to mass-mind thinking about drafts causing chills, wet feet, etc.; feeling sorry for oneself.

There is no past, present, and future to God. Evil never enters into the being or experience of God. Our mind must come to know and realize these truths if we are to have a real and lasting peace.

Remember that these causes of illness are only guidelines. Do not forget that Jesus referred to several possible causes for diseases other than wrong thinking including karmic conditions and those given to you for "the glory of God." Also, remember that Jesus taught you to judge with righteous judgment and not by what appears to be. Disease and illness teach you to maintain an appropriate balance in your thinking and the physical world. We should not object to any of the forms of healing available today. Physicians often do marvelous work and deserve our gratitude. But, no form of cure will be permanent until our thought pattern is healed.

You can apply your understanding of the law to all aspects of your life. You can use it to change your financial situation. You can use it to affect your relationships, and bring about a better life in all ways. Some people have been taught that one should not pray for one's own needs. Jesus never taught that. He said that we should ask for whatever we want or need, and it will be given to us. He told us that it is God's good pleasure to give us the whole kingdom, because God loves us. God gives us the means, through the law, and gives us the guidelines of what to take into account while doing so through the teachings of Jesus and Mary. Then God sets us free to create as we wish.

Remember, the invisible world is real and has power over the material, visible world. Only we can keep us from the love of God. The energy that creates the newly conceived fetus in a mother's womb is the same force that gives us our paycheck. What you believe about people you must believe and accept about God. You receive what you can accept through the law. We need to take responsibility for what we have made of our lives. If we don't like the results of the choices we made, we need to make a different choice.

THE LAW III

The law not only works in the material world, but also works in the subtler realms. There, it attracts to us personal and interpersonal experiences that will be harmonious or inharmonious based on whether we are putting out positive or negative energy. Each of us has an atmosphere that has been formed by all we have thought, felt, said, and done either consciously or subconsciously. Our atmosphere determines what we will attract to ourselves. Children and animals are very sensitive to people's atmosphere, being drawn to those who are inwardly good and repelled by those who are inwardly negative. The atmosphere of a place contains all the actions, emotions and thoughts expressed by the people who inhabit it. Did you ever go somewhere where the people who live there did not want you there and it made you so uncomfortable that you wanted to leave? On the other hand, how often have you sometimes felt such a warm inner glow when you went to a new place that you wanted to stay? The atmosphere of our home should be filled with peace and love so that the negation of the world does not enter there. Negative emotions, like anger, mistrust, doubt and worry make things so unpleasant that everyone feels depressed living there. The negative energy must be replaced with love, compassion, patience and tenderness towards others.

The atmosphere of the desert, uninhabited mountains, or in the middle of a lake or ocean is wonderful and free from thoughts of confusion or fear. Anything that has happened in the past on this planet is recorded in the atmosphere today and can be picked up by sensitive people right now. Everybody radiates some kind of vibration at all times. So we are surrounded by an atmosphere called an aura, extending a few inches to a few feet, sometimes even farther from the body. In moments of spiritual illumination, a person's atmosphere is a bright light, almost golden white color. When we are angry, our atmosphere clouds with darkness. We can learn to have our atmosphere screen out any and all things that we do not want to come into us. There is a more pronounced radiation around the head than around the rest of the body and that produces the halo that some people have been able to see around the heads of saints. The face of Jesus sometimes shone so brightly that disciples could not look upon it without being blinded by his brilliance. Many of the saints have seen Jesus because they have studied his works and words so much that they completely entered his thought and thus have been able to see an image of him. It doesn't follow that all of them actually have seen Jesus, but they have seen a vivid mental likeness of him, or have unmistakably perceived his presence and being. Others have seen Jesus himself as a result of Jesus' decision to present himself to someone.

We are immortal. That means we continue to exist and be alive as a soul after the experience of death. We carry our feelings, thoughts, memories, experiences, desires and habits with us into the next life. At times we can communicate and be communicated with and are able to be seen and understood by others after we have left our bodies.

We have complete memory of all of our lives. What we are today is the result of all the experiences of our many lives. When we make the transition from this life to the spiritual world, we have all of our experiences and tendencies intact. Jesus appeared to his disciples after his resurrection, to demonstrate to them the victory over death. Death is just a passage to a higher sphere. The level of spiritual attainment we have worked for in this life will determine the out-of-the-body experience that we have earned. If we are not in a heavenly state when we die, meaning in continuous relationship with God, we will not automatically graduate to Heaven, where God is always present, when we pass over. Leaving the flesh body is not a guarantee of graduating into

Heaven. We don't attain immortality. We already are immortal.

What is a Mystic? A mystic is not a mysterious person. A mystic has a deep inner experience of God within and they feel connected to the life of God. They are one with the whole and intuitively perceive truth in profound Self Realization. What are some of the truths mystics have taught?

1. There is but one ultimate reality, which is here now. We can be an embodiment of this oneness.

2. There is a personal God that can be known, seen, heard and felt. God is not anthropomorphic having human form, but God is consciously working in us and through us.

3. Having been illumined by the Christ light, and seen through the veil of matter into the very Self of God, and perceived the spiritual universe, mystics have taught that the Kingdom of God is present now and can be realized.

4. Evil is not an ultimate reality but simply an experience of the soul on its journey toward reality. Evil is an unfortunate misuse of the one power of God for destructive and selfish ends. Evil is anything that separates us from God.

5. Salvation is possible for everyone. The soul is immortal. Damnation is not conceivable to the mystic just as any belief in evil is to the mind of God.

6. We should have no problems and would not have any, if we turned to God. In Matthew 11:29 Jesus said, **"Come to me all you who labor and are heavy laden, and I will give you rest."**

7. We live in one life. **"For in God we live, and move, and have our being."**

8. The real Self is God which resides in the center of our being. It is the total soul expression through all lifetimes.

9. The soul is returning to its Father's house. In Psalms 82:6 it says, **"You are gods; and all of you are children of the Most High."**

10. Intuition in human beings (similar to instinct in animals) guides us if we will allow it to operate through us, or from the God Self.

Mystics are regular people, living in the world in a perfectly natural way. They do not cloak themselves in mystery. Some of them do not even know they are mystics until they are forced to acknowledge this fact by their experiences. It is difficult to describe what a mystic experiences, and may be very difficult to believe the reports of what they see. They see reality in a flash which illuminates their whole being, and they see light so brilliant that they are sometimes blinded for as long as several days. Illumination can come as we more and more realize our unity with the Whole and as we constantly endeavor to let the light operate through us. We should seek to emulate the mystics, by turning within to find God at the center of our being. The times will come when everyone will seek to solve their problems through the power and the light of the Spirit.

When we experience Self Realization, we merge with God in a loving embrace that is so deep and powerful, that we lose identification with our body, mind and emotions. We do not lose our essential personality or our soul. Meditation becomes the means through which union with God continues and grows as the voice of the silence becomes clearly audible.

Then we truly enact what is written in Isaiah 60:1 where God says, **"Arise; shine, for your light is come."** When we become one with the great God-Self within as developed sons and daughters of God, we can say with God, **"I am that I am."** (Exodus 3:14)

GRACE

In the New Testament, grace is called the work of faith and knowing. It is the force of action working through grace. In nature we see it in the progressive growth and development of plants in their seasonal cycles. We see it in the increasing speed of movement in a tornado and its reappearance in another place.

As we pass through successive incarnations, generally, we start the new cycle at a little higher level of life. Remember the sayings: "There is a little good in everyone," and "There are no bad boys." Well, this is true. Grace is what we would call in the mechanical world "momentum." In other words, we move mentally and spiritually at a certain rate of development and we do not have to make an effort to do this; but due to the action of grace, we accomplish a little more than what we make the effort to do.

Our faith in knowing that the law works sets up a momentum that carries us along. Let us liken our life and actions to that of a business person. They deposit so much money in a checking account and a certain amount in savings which draws interest. The checking account does not create interest. The same is true if you live in accord with the law of creation. We watch our thinking and speech each day. We pray and meditate each day to develop our consciousness and also get rid of any negative conditions or illness. We receive the money, supply or other things we need in our life.

Daily prayer for daily needs is something that balances us and creates a force to invoke grace. Training our thinking, keeping our thoughts positive and watching the words we use, this is what builds up a reserve balance and invokes grace. Prayer is the most effective means of making a permanent contact with God, the thing that builds a perpetual subconscious function.

Thus we will have complied with the first commandment, **"You shall have no other gods before me."**

The laws of nature are so easy to work with if we get our bloated egos out of the way. Then life becomes a simple and a beautiful thing.

Grace means we always get more from God than we put in. Why? Well, let us take an example of a woman using the law of prayer to heal a pain or arthritis. When she uses the law, she is bound to get rid of other minor imperfections along with the arthritis. Thus we receive the interest from our bank account with God.

All things are in accord with cosmic law. Forces ordained by the Creator are in operation, whether we know it or not. That star up there, many millions of miles away, is influencing the cells in our physical bodies.

In 1st Peter 1:13 it says, **"Therefore free your minds of limitations; be sober and discipline yourselves; hope to the end for the grace that will be brought to you at the revelation of Jesus Christ."** In 1st Peter 4:10, the Apostle Peter asked the people to be good stewards in service to one another, using whatever gifts they may have received, dispensing the grace of God in its varied forms. So this grace is a gift that God bestows to each of us according to how God wants it. Grace comes to aid in the transformation of the old person weighed down by sins into the new person with the body of light. Thus is the soul transformed. Grace is the free, unmerited and unearned love of God that moves us toward salvation. There is no particular action on our part that causes the grace to come to us, but the action arises from God's will and decision. Romans 11:6 reads, **"And if by grace, then it is no more by works."** Thus we did not earn this by being good or by obeying all the rules, for Paul says again in Romans

5:20, **"Where sin abounded, grace did much more abound."**

Those who do not know what Jesus brought need the grace more because they would have no way to salvation without this hope. Since they did not follow the path of good works which God ordained for those under the law of Moses, the path of the disciple following the wisdom of Jesus Christ and Mother Mary was a more excellent way. It is through the grace and truth of Jesus that we unite ourselves to God, as was taught in the ancient wisdom schools.

Therefore, in Romans 6:14 Paul writes, **"You are not under the Law, but under grace."** For the way of the law has been too hard for the undisciplined. They could not, or would not, go this way because it was in such conflict with the mind of the world. Rather than see humanity destroyed by their own hardness of heart and negativity, the Creator sent His Son to teach and heal them. The effort that God made was similar to that of leading someone out of a burning building that would have destroyed them. God actually led them out of the burning city and told them to not look back, just like God told Lot.

Jesus, our Master, was offering His safety, sent directly as the Son of God. God sent him as a King would send his crown prince to handle important problems too complicated for the King's other ministers. Grace may also come through exhilaration, and consistent use of the law becoming a personal attribute of our personality. As we unite with God and become one with God, we draw down grace which moves us along into wisdom. Attaining this state of unity becomes the acting mechanism of our being and now our entire state of existence is the acceptance and release of the law that causes the Spirit to manifest our word.

Jesus never used the word 'grace' in the New Testament, but Paul used it repeatedly. Jesus Christ brought grace and forgiveness, and the Holy Spirit brought it to Paul so he could teach it to disciples. Paul received grace on his way to Damascus because of his love for God, even though he was surprised to find he was persecuting Jesus Christ which was against God. This is what Jesus Christ does to us on our journey to God. Paul was startled and shaken by a blinding and overpowering light on the road to Damascus. And then, when he had time to digest the importance of this miracle, Christ built a new Paul over the old. The old was burned out and the new one poured in, only the form looked the same. Grace imparts strength to endure the trial and helps us resist temptation. The Sacraments are channels of grace and demonstrate the grace they represent.

Grace proceeds from the Virgin Mary and is part of the feminine aspect and the desire to give birth. The miracle of conception and birth are made possible through the grace of God, increasing our fullness and supply. The generation of new things comes under the dominion of grace. The fullness of grace that descended upon the Virgin Mary at the announcement of the Archangel Gabriel, caused her to conceive of the Holy Spirit. God was conceived within her. She became the living Ark of the Covenant, the first human being who manifested such purity and obedience to the Creator that she was given the gift, the grace, of being the first one to consciously carry the Christ within her body. That experience was the highest grace ever given by God to a human being. Mary took on the grace of God so fully that she came to be called "The Full of Grace." She became the grace itself.

When we eat at the dinner table, we say grace. This is a prayer of blessing and thanksgiving that acknowledges God as the source of supply. Grace means a dispensation and a favor given to us by the Creator. Grace is a response from God granting us a favor, good will, gratitude, virtue or individual excellence. When a priest uses the words, "I absolve you," the person is restored to grace, much like in Baptism, where the water brings grace to the soul to wash clean and forgive sins so we can start the spiritual path consciously.

In John 1:14-17 writes, **"And the Word was made flesh and lived among us. We have seen the glory which is his as the only Son of God, full of grace and truth."** Here the Apostle connects grace with love, for Jesus said that love fulfills the law, the law as it was given by Moses. And it was the grace and truth that love brought that became our salvation. Grace is developed by practicing the fruits of the spirit: love, patience, kindness, generosity, faithfulness, gentleness and self-control. The fruits of the spirit bring grace as well as the regeneration of the physical body.

THE WAY I

Jesus Christ, the great Avatar and Master, who is spoken of in the New Testament as the Lord of Earth, said, **"I am the Way, the Truth and the Life."** This is probably one of the most profound statements of all times.

All religions, orders, mystical and spiritual schools lead to the same path of intersection, the way, which is the path of initiation. All eventually get there and find a new freedom and reality of life. Religions, philosophies and science have the goal of ennobling human beings. Each aspiration lifts us out of the realm of a purely physical existence and leads us toward freedom. Most churches have a philosophical background that may include some dogmatic teachings, and in so far as they live up to their true function, they can prepare people to follow their beliefs and experience some of the reality.

On the way all dogmas, beliefs and philosophies are either perfect or less perfect expressions of the functioning Word of God. In the teachings of Jesus, we have a handbook describing the solar initiations that are possible for each of us to go through if we prepare ourselves. When we seek to put our feet on the way we become the channel through which the light of Christ functions. We become co-operators with this great creative mind and power.

Historically, we have noticed that some people stand out. Some were classified as mystics by the masses, some as teachers, priests, missionaries, or carriers of the Word. It was the peace and love of these people that attracted people to them. Was there something these mystics were endowed with that other people did not have and were not able to get? No. The Creator endowed all of us alike. Each had the same opportunity to learn and use their powers. Each was provided with the same reality of atonement, and each had the same tools. It's just that some knew how to use them better than others. Some had discovered their true nature as sons or daughters of God while others had not found it yet. They were all alike in that they made up their minds that manifesting the divine was more important than anything else in life. They decided that God was the most important thing to experience.

It is our endeavor to take the mystery out of the Mysteries so that the teachings of Jesus Christ will be real to you. Most of the teachings can be taught to everyone with the exception of the higher teachings that are only taught to the priesthood. The way is truly a universal pattern of soul growth. In simple language, the way is the ultimate path of attainment to travel to peace, understanding, and love. This is the way, the path that all have to follow. It is the underlying path described and directed by the Creator. It is what Jesus Christ, our Master, demonstrated while here on earth, when he took himself through the initiation of crucifixion and resurrection. It is the path that all great ones travel on the earth.

We have no new philosophy. We simply unite the teachings of Jesus with the supporting wisdom teachings of the ancient mystery schools. The outstanding difference between what we are doing and the doctrine of the conventional churches is that we are interested in the existing powers in the universe and how they work. There are a number of schools that teach part of these things, but have not united them in one cosmic pattern. To be a real disciple involves the same thing taught by many great teachers. It is the art of really accepting the light, finding the Self, and understanding the Self, so you can understand others. Seeing the Self and working with the Self will allow you to truly know another and know that you too are not different, even though you may never wholly agree on different points due to your different experiences.

When we understand this, we will be able to accept the different ways in which we are manifesting God's energy in our station in the stream of life. Even the person who tries to do us harm, cannot harm us bodily or spiritually. If we know the power we possess, we will understand what motivates their negative action and will ask for protection. After all, they are the ones who are going to pay for it. We say, "Don't kick against the pricks, just flow along over them." Remember, no one is going to put anything over on you unless you think they can. And further, who can get away with anything? Work toward the way through real discipleship, live with us, and grow with us in this age of beauty. Help us share the great truths that have been hidden, the truths that so many are so hungry for. We knowingly started our involution into dense matter, and are now starting our evolution out, to attain our Godhood or Self-mastery.

For centuries the Eastern schools published widely about the spiritual attainment of illumination and Realization. In this lesson, we will unveil the mystery behind the words illumination, Realization, Mastery and Ascension. Nothing we teach is contradictory to the teachings of the Master Jesus, Buddha, or any of the great avatars who have come to earth to bring us the greatness and the glory of the Creator. God's means of expression and God's greatest satisfaction is the creation of human beings.

ILLUMINATION
After we have accomplished the experience of conscious mystical Baptism, and have given ourselves over to the service of God, we find ourselves entering the experience of the illumination. When we no longer possess things in the material world, and we are not obsessed by them, we have accomplished what the Bible talks about as giving up the world and all things in it. This does not mean we should give away our house, sell our car, deny our children or our wife, put on sackcloth and go out and walk the highways teaching the impoverished Jesus Christ.

Jesus Christ was not an impoverished being. He wore the very best of clothing, the seamless garment, which was in reality a garment woven without seams and was very expensive. Most of the time, Jesus did not stop in a town and live with beggars or the poor. He spent the night with average people, artisans and workers. We can hear you say, **"But the Master said it was harder for a rich person to enter the kingdom of heaven than for a camel to pass through the needle's eye."** You are absolutely right, for the eye of the needle was a small arch, an opening through a great rock, too small and too low for the camel to walk through. In order for the caravan to pass, it was necessary that as each camel came to the opening; their loads of merchandise and wares were unpacked. The camel had to get on its knees and waddle through, and was re-saddled with its load, and proceeded on into Jerusalem. This is a most profound allegory, and yet a true story in the New Testament.

For anyone seeking illumination, it is necessary for them to give up their material load, forget their burden and errors of the past, to humble themselves before their teacher or priest, and to pass through certain experiences that they might think are not entirely fitting, before they are able to again stand on their feet, and walk in the way, on the way to Jerusalem. The mystical interpretation of Jerusalem, while being an actual location on the map, is the human vehicle and its spiritual vehicles. Therefore, it is necessary that we go into Jerusalem in order to gain greater wisdom, and to really find the light.

When we use the term "light," we mean Light, not understanding. It takes self-discipline and a certain amount of informative instruction in order for the seeker of illumination to be able to know what they are looking for. If I am filled with the light, what will it do? What will it accomplish? How does light conceivably help me in finding eternal life?" And we say this to you: All the Christed ones who have experienced the real light and illumination, and there are some among us today, see light in their body in meditation. Perhaps without knowing it, you have seen people who shine even in the dark, and in reality they do. These people get answers to their prayers and they gain wisdom from God inside them, not in some allegorical or abstract way. Many hear a voice, some see the words actually put in front of them, some hear distinctly, within their own being, the answer. It comes in different forms, but it is all concise, and unmistakably received and known.

These faculties are not a special thing given to just special people. These are earned faculties and must be acquired through distinctive desire and realizing that the first commandment comes first. Then we discipline ourselves and gain the wisdom, and with the help of our teacher, gain these faculties. Truth is the personality of God. Truth is the gift of God to God's most cherished possession, human beings. We should proceed step by step toward the great light of Christ within. But we should not be held back because we do not have any money. Money seems to be the commodity that seems so frequently to be the yardstick of how much of the truth we may learn.

Our soul is here for the purpose of directing, controlling, and perfecting the evolution of the physical body and personality. It is also here for the elimination of all traits of character that interfere with a broad, universal comprehension insuring cosmic attunement. Cosmic attunement is the feeling of God in your being and knowing that it is there. We acknowledge a superior power and personality of God in creation, which we adore with our very fiber. We can only attain this real knowing of God by renouncing the confusion and frustration of the world consciousness, by disciplining the body, mind and emotions. The Master Jesus referred to this humility by warning against vainglorious indulgence in wealth that satisfies the pride and the lower self.

The fiery soul, pure, clear gold and tested in the fire of the Holy Spirit of God is the husband of the noble Sophia - for she is the very tincture of light. This is the attainment of our Holy Marriage with the Holy Spirit. We do not lose our personality through rebirth. This spiritual marriage with the inner being occurs at Self Realization. We are reborn and our consciousness is united with the very consciousness of God, the very center and core of this universe. Only in this way can we become who we were created to be, an immortal soul and universal personality. This is what the Master Jesus meant when he said, **"Blessed are the pure in heart, for they shall see God."** He meant every word.

He also said, **"Behold, the bridegroom comes; go forth to meet him."** That Light comes to us only after the obscure night passes, and sometimes the very blackness of events have taken place in our lives. We seem to need to be beaten to the dust to experience the crucifixion and death like Jesus did on the cross at Golgotha. The Master Jesus experienced this when He said, **"My God, my God, why have you forsaken me?"** This is sometimes our condition when we give up the world and receive our salvation, either consciously or unconsciously.

But so much more power is brought into our being and made accessible through the action of the light.

THE WAY II

We want to talk about the afterlife and Heaven and Hell because the whole Christian teaching points to a life hereafter. It is evident in reading the Bible that our way of life on earth, our conduct, thoughts and words are our passport to the life hereafter. The state of consciousness that we attain here on earth determines the life we will be prepared to live in the spiritual world and also the kind of life we will incarnate into when we return to earth. Our actions here also determine the joy and glories we will experience while we are in the heaven world. Do not be misled by the term "state of consciousness," because heaven is a real place.

The initiations of illumination and Self Realization are a way to prepare ourselves for the experience on the other side. Many revelations were received to prepare the student/disciple for the development of this consciousness. The initiations are a way that we can have all the tools that Jesus told us about for our use here on earth. Bringing others into the light and illumination is the principle objective of this work. Attaining the light serves as a purifying agent of the soul, and has a tremendous effect on our life after transition. It aids us to attain a higher level of life in the next cycle than the one we just finished.

Our Master Jesus Christ preached repentance from the start of his ministry, and did so consistently all through his ministry. It has been said that the eyes are the windows of the soul. This is why it has been found that if something is amiss in the body, the eyes will not clear until the body is well again. This is the reason why Christians should always be interested in soul purification. The purity of the soul will allow the gleaming light of the Self to show through. Soul purity is an indispensable part of gaining repentance.

It is our endeavor to bring each person into the light of Christ, and thus pave the way in a substantial way for their salvation. Receiving the real light is the manifestation of God's greatest love for a human soul.

The soul has a personal friend who is a guardian and member of God's court. This guardian has the duty to guard our soul, as it is said that the Son of Man came to save every soul as a shepherd rescues the lost sheep. We seek to bring the light of Christ to everyone, thus purifying the body. The purpose of this effort to purify the soul is so that when the body passes through transition and the soul and Self leave the body, we may rise to a higher level. We will experience a higher consciousness of what we are doing if we are prepared than if our soul purification had not been attended by a teacher or priest.

Jesus said, **"I go to prepare a place for you. In my Father's house are many mansions, and if it were not so I would have told you."**

For a long time priests, ministers, and theologians have tried to destroy or avoid the reality of the teachings of Jesus Christ. In their avoidance, they have led people to the edge of a precipice of darkness and void, scaring some people a great deal. Some have taught that death is the end of existence itself. The time has come for us to really know. We cannot join the authors and theologians who pacify, deter, cast down to a lower level and destroy the reality of God which Jesus was talking about before his resurrection. We can say positively that Heaven is real. You can call it anything you want. It is another realm, another place, another level of vibration just as real as the one we live in. It is less dense than that of earth, but it is still real and you are there when you leave the earth plane. If you're soul and Self, your experience and vibration, are high enough and clean enough, then you will go there.

When you are there it is just as real as your present world is to you today, and just as real as breakfast and muffins.

You won't find streets paved with gold. You won't have to use a pick or a shovel, but you are going to have to use your mind to control your vehicle. Your efforts in concentration, contemplation and other spiritual exercises will be an asset to you when you start to function with the reality of the soul and Self. You will find the simple exercises that you were asked to do on earth will bring you comfort in the world hereafter, as your conscious desire enables you to function there.

It is very difficult for Christians to go into any state of contemplation or reach beyond the barrier between this world and the next to gain firsthand information of God's reality. The spiritual world is above us in that it is less dense and higher in vibration. We are talking about a real place. We have to be careful that we don't strain to become so technologically accurate about creation that we ignore the unseen world. There is more to the unseen world than to the seen. It is vital that we learn something about the place we are preparing to travel to.

Are the theologians correct? Are the mystics who experienced heaven really heretics as the Christian churches accused them? The churches judged the mystics and saints who knew God as a reality and persecuted them as evildoers and tools of the devil. Isn't it true that they were only looking in the mirror? The time has come to forget Christianity and remember God and Jesus Christ and how they built this creation. These lessons are about a real God, which would still be heresy today.

Heaven is a state of consciousness. When you can raise your vibration so that you can participate on that higher level, you will be able to go to Heaven. According to the level to which you have been able to raise your consciousness, you will be able to move in that higher sphere of life either on earth or in heaven.

As we move closer to the reality of the Christos, or to Christ, increasingly we take on the consciousness and greater reality of the life of the whole of this solar system. We arrive at the experience of worlds within worlds and wheels within wheels. The closer we get to the Christos, the higher will we rise in vibration and the purer will we become. God can only experience through our actions and thus gain the joy of the denser world. We call this state cosmic consciousness. Each person has some part of this consciousness, but few are totally conscious of this whole in an earth body, except Jesus Christ and Mother Mary. This is on the scale of the totality of God.

If you let go of iniquity, sins, or errors, as you raise the totality of your life pattern and function and grow closer to Jesus Christ and the Mother Mary, the Masters of this Earth, you will be able to move up in the heaven world when you leave the dense body behind.

The reason for the initiation of illumination is so that, as Jesus said: **"If your eye be single, your body will be full of light."** As the physical body fills with light and the regeneration starts to carry you through, then you will move toward a point of complete illumination where the dense body is no longer dense. You may experience the ascension as the Master Jesus and Mother Mary did. You will conquer death and it will no longer be part of you. You will have become a universal soul and know the Masters in a more personal way. This gives us the freedom of a continuous life as eternal servants of our Creator. We will not have to return and incarnate in a material body unless we so desire in order to perform a mission, or on some other orb to aid God in the work of raising people in some other world.

Heaven and hell really exist. We can skip the psychic world and not pay any attention to it except to guard yourself against its negation and those who inhabit there. When you come into training, you are told to let go and let God. We instruct you to forget the past and look just to the present. Then sometimes you try to hang on to little things or bad habits that you like. You can't quite make up your mind to make a final commitment and give all to the Master, because of one or a number of human frailties. Then your teacher will instruct you to get on one side of the fence or the other. You can't attain the initiations of illumination and God Realization while you are on the fence. You have to make up your mind.

The student is preparing themself for service and initiation. If they are sincerely following the path of Jesus and Mary and looking forward to life in the heaven world where they will be close to the Host and can be taught by them and can enjoy life without the heaviness of the physical body, then they will move right on up. If we keep our eye on the Masters and the heaven world and do not pay any attention to those psychic things between, then those things will not affect us. But if we become too dense and are not able to function in the heaven world, then we will find ourselves at the time we go through transition, in the borderland where we may not see the face of the Creator or our Masters Jesus and Mary.

The lower part of this level of vibration is the borderland. If we are too densely steeped in material life we may become earthbound. If we have committed heinous crimes, according to the Creator, we may find ourselves in a vibrationless non-existence, or hell. The much-talked-of fires of hell are our desires for the multitude of things which we have previously experienced or the desire for communication with others, the wanting to be known, the desire for food and drink, and many others, which create a terrific flame of hell.

Hell is the negative side, the absence of light and complete resistance to it, experienced often on earth as one is being purged of error. Hell is for those who hate God and have decided not to come close to God. As the dross is being burned away and is ignited, you can't stay under the influences of the light, and the pain is from the intense heat. If there are impurities left on the soul after coming into illumination or passing over, there is a constant burning. The territory that the church calls purgatory covers the psychic and the desire world, or the lower levels of the heaven world. As psychic stuff is the flesh of the spiritual body, if you have any impurities, you will feel the psychic world when you pass through.

THE WAY III

We often see things the way we want to see them instead of how they really are. Even when we find the path of initiation we think we really have something, but it is only our imagination because we are conceptualizing it instead of experiencing it. When we really step on the way, it is very real and our life becomes very different from what it was before. We will learn to meditate on the Christ light, for light opens the door drawing us to the fullness of the Creator, filling every part of our being.

In working with the light, students begin to see a great deal of blue light when they look within. We have ventured into the realm of the Self and will see the blue light that emanates there. One of the great teachers of India, Lord Krishna, said that renunciation was a state between our world and the real world. In it there existed a strange haze which he called the veil of the gods. People would say that Krishna was not of this world but of heaven, which was right. For the Creator did not give Krishna power to keep a physical body on earth so he could teach people, but it was given by higher beings that nothing in nature could harm the spirit of Krishna. Krishna was very powerful and was called the god of love, which was his message to people on earth. He was also called the Blue God because he was forever surrounded by the blue veil of initiation.

The blue veil that one sees near the time of Self Realization is the same blue we see in the sky. The Sun seems frosted in the deep blue of outer space, sometime appearing as almost black. This is the veil of the gods, which is always around those who have consciously taken on the state of immortality. Perhaps the term "etheric" may be applied to the new race, which would be in the blue spectrum. It is said in India that Krishna was superior to all living things, and that he belonged to a mystic race whose bodies were formed of a deep blue spiritual ether like the heavens.

Every true teacher has reached a certain stage of development where there is a veil between them and the world. They walk among us but they are not of the world. With material eyes it is hard to see this veil, the blue veil. But with spiritual sight we can see it as a barrier dividing us from those who have not passed behind this veil. Some people are behind the red haze of materiality, and others, who have experienced spiritual illumination, are behind the shining veil. We feel drawn to some people in spite of ourselves, while there are those we don't feel drawn to at all, who are miles away in another spiritual temperament.

There are those whom you would not slap on the back though they are your best friend. A power surrounds them, a wall you cannot penetrate. There is a respect, an attitude, that one feels they are different. There are those who have given their life in the priesthood, who serve everyone, yet you cannot seem to know them, notwithstanding their love for people. They have reached the point where they are not in this world, nor of this world, and there is a veil between them and others that cannot be pierced.

Only those who pass with renunciation and simplicity behind the veil can understand the true impact of the difference between the false and the true. Like the joy of self-forgetting service, most people do not understand this unless they have experienced the initiations. When you have just come through the world of initiation, coming into a new state of being you are, at this point a stranger in a strange new land. Those seeking peace, rest, and personal comfort will find agony awaiting them; but those who come seeking service, which is the keynote of their being, will experience heaven and great joy.

Jesus said, **"Take up your cross and follow me."** That wall that separates the initiated from the uninitiated is as real as consciousness itself. To the uninitiated, it does not seem to exist at all. To those who have passed behind it, it is more solid than the densest granite and more resistant than the strongest steel, and thousands have battered themselves against this wall of God. But only those who are like a little child may enter in. Sometimes when you are out of your body, you may happen against this wall, but in spite of all your power you cannot pass. You are drawn back time after time. When you are ready to see behind it, you are changed as you pass through.

Occasionally, we meet one who is called master and is of a different grade of consciousness. Once we have seen the great truth, we do not forget it, and can never be one again with ignorance, which we left behind. For the material joys we once experienced no longer fascinate us and the ways we used to spend our time now pass as foolishness. It is our own life that divided us from the world. When we become an intelligent worker in the great plan, we have great joy and mutual love with other souls on the way.

A person who has not developed properly presents a very difficult problem. They want to go forward, and sometimes they forget that in passing through the veil by the sheer weight of the arts they have learned, they pass through to put the blue wall between them and the life they have lived. Because they have forced themselves by impure desires, they take steps that are not in tune with the world. They have passed behind the veil not in sweet simplicity and devotion, but in great determination to get things that they should not have in their present condition. They are as if dead to the earth, for by the force of their actions and mentality, they forced a result that may be agonizing to them spiritually, physically and mentally. For they have become citizens of another world. The confusion caused by forcing things is often too much for them.

We must be workers with higher motives, having made a sacred choice. We have renounced the material world and the craving for things as we once knew them. Yet if we want the world and crave what we cannot be a part of, we will suffer. In obsession, some have reached a position halfway through the veil. They have aspired to heaven while tied to earth. A terrible rupture of the organism is the only result of such a path. We must learn renunciation not only of mind but of spirit. Until we do give up all things freely of ourselves, we are in hell. If we desire heaven and still crave sensual gratification, we will be confused and we will suffer.

Remember, you cannot get away from that which you really are. You must build on a solid foundation of harmonized growth. Many become imbalanced through undisciplined study. How many Cleopatras, Napoleons and Julius Ceasars have you met? People learn a little about reincarnation and then twist it with their own imaginations. There is a natural unfoldment of information about who we were; but what is most important is who you are now and what you do and think here.

Are you one of those students who picture yourself sitting on a throne somewhere playing a harp, and at the same time trying to stifle your desire for ice cream? If you are, stop subjugating your desires by strength of will which can never be fully satisfying or effective. Take on the image of Christ by patterning your life after him and be yourself instead of imagining how you would like yourself to be. Don't be divided between your ideals and your cravings when you are seeking initiation, for you will only preserve the selfish traits and find a hell within them. Let go and let God, and accept God's way.

For those who have penetrated the veil, there is no problem at all. But if you have not let go and you seek to take on a real spiritual initiation, you may damage your physical body and may not move forward. You have to be through with the things you left behind, because now things of the spirit come first. Your first waking thought must be of God and your greatest joy, prayer. You cannot ascend to the higher states of vibration of being carrying prejudices, likes, dislikes and temper. Many may pray in the morning, concentrate at midday and meditate in the evening, while the rest of the time they show the meanest character they could to people around them. Many people practice nothing and force their attainment through will.

"Be of good cheer. Take up your rod and your staff - your cross - and follow me, and I will give you rest," said our Lord Jesus.

GUIDELINES

1. It is not what is written in a lesson that teaches you, but it is what is stimulated in you that brings you to truth.

2. Keep on the way; never look back and never run. If you think, you cannot be receptive to the Creator.

3. The mind is the dreamer on the threshold and it has helped to create that dreamer. It will try to keep you so busy that you will not get a chance to look across that threshold or enter it. The teacher's needlessness becomes the need of the individual student.

4. If you do the things you are given, the initiations will start. But you will not get anywhere until you begin to live them. Light brings light into the darkness; but darkness brings darkness, not light.

261

5. Always be positive, not timid, for timidity is not humility. For in humility is great power.

6. Remember, meditation is not the pastime of weaklings but the workbench of masters, where things are created in the image of God.

7. All is in the mind of God, except what we miscreated.

8. Virginity does not give chastity; chastity is in the spirit.

9. Light is the password that opens doors.

10. If you pray too much you infer doubt on the first prayer, creating a new doubt, and have to pray about that. But if you pray constantly you have but one prayer and there is no doubt.

11. Prayer is mental, vocal and through positive action.

12. It requires light to find safe and sound Realization of the Self. When Jesus said: "Sell all you have and follow me," He meant to get rid of all the assumptions and ideas you have and not to keep one foot on the fence. In other words, you don't forget your service and obedience, not only to your teacher, but also to God. You had better be obedient, giving yourself in service completely.

13. To want not only to journey but also to arrive, nothing helps but the will to go, but to will vigorously and wholeheartedly, not to turn and toss this way and that. A struggling will, one part leading and the other following, is a person who has not given all to the Creator.

14. We are all seeking entrance to the path, every mystic student, every adept, every seeker advances desiring to enter. Each has heard of the way.

THE WAY IV

In John 14, Jesus says, **"Let not your hearts be troubled. Believe in God, believe also in me. In my Father's house are many rooms. If it were not so, I would have told you. I go to prepare a place for you. And if I go and prepare a place for you, I will come again and will take you to myself, so that where I am, there you may be also. And where I go you know and the way you know. Thomas said to Jesus, 'Lord, we do not know where you are going. How can we know the way?' Jesus said to him, "I am the Way, and the Truth, and the Life. No one comes to God except through me. If you know me, you will know my Father also. From this moment on you know God and have seen God."**

This is a description of the totality of the approach to the way. The mystic path is the path of light. This is the secret of all life, treasure and being. Only through gaining the light of Christ within and having the door opened to the Self can you reach a point of simplicity. When you become nothing, then you can become the all. This is the fire of life that warms us, gives us birth, and gives us Life. This is the Yod, the divine flame that brings the regeneration. It is the way to Godhood, where each of you can attain the reality of all.

There is a difference between your life as it was and the life you experience after you make a decision to live on the way. There was a time when you just went along with life as it was. Then you came to a place where all things turned dark. This was an inevitable process in which you came to what felt like nothing and you couldn't go anywhere except through it. This tested your faith more than anything else. People go through many troubles and difficulties because they have not been taught to take these changing experiences in stride. The great anguish you feel sometimes in moving along the spiritual path is normal and necessary in order to experience the crucifixion as Jesus did. When you see that you are going through something and you have the knowledge that this is some kind of spiritual change or initiation, don't fight it. Don't think that it is someone putting some kind of heavy burden on you or that Jesus or God has laid a hand on you to make you suffer. That is the conventional church approach to handling problems and trials that come along in the material world. That won't work. Many of the difficulties we experience happen in a very orderly manner, even though they seem to you to be problems. But most of our work in teaching you is to help you realize that you do not have any problems. The things you are experiencing are some form of initiation and you should not let them bother you. They are part of the real drama of the spiritual life.

It is not Jesus reaching down and putting you through something because you didn't handle something perfectly. That is a total misconception about the way things really work. The Christian churches have failed to teach the reality of the truth, much less do they know how to guide a person through these experiences. The Mass is a sacrament enacting the drama of the Lord's Supper. A priest, when performing the Mass, sacrifices themselves into the shadow, form, and image of Jesus Christ and Mother Mary, taking them on as a reality. Then the bread and wine are transformed into the body and the blood. The churches will not teach this, so they put people through troubles which would otherwise be joyful experiences. People would be happy to experience these things and would not mind the trials if they knew the experience would help them grow spiritually.

Many people feel that the problems of the present day are the most difficult in history. Today's problems are different in nature and require differing solutions than in the past. The new heaven and earth is coming, not the end of the human race. It may be the end for those who do not learn to use the creative force and power and who fail to experience the realization of this great consciousness. It is absolutely necessary for each of you to be conscious of your smallness in order to become conscious of your greatness. How can you become that god unless you become conscious of the greatness of your reality?

If you will take a close look at the different religions, you will notice that each one stresses some particular point of the teachings of the Master Jesus, or whichever Avatar they follow. Some stress the Holy Spirit, some reincarnation, some the forgiveness of sins, and some the laying on of hands. In most cases, what they teach is taken from the scriptures and is good. But usually, they do not teach all the necessary tools that you need to attain and really put your feet upon the way. You are left adrift when you are not given the tools to build your temple and prepare for the life after you are out of your body. In other words, most people do not get the whole story and many ministers have withheld the truth from the believers. The mysteries were hidden from the majority of people because it was felt that they could not understand them and would misuse them. These mysteries contain the tools you must understand and use in order to build the body of light and really be able to be of service to God.

The passage in the Bible that states, **"Prepare, for the bridegroom comes,"** is what the priests and ministers should be helping people with who are getting ready for the experience of the light of Christ. They should have the answers and should know these things. You should know the world you live in, the law of prayer, the basic laws of creation and how to create with those laws. You must be conscious of the unseen, as well as the seen world. You will be able to see those things that people usually do not see, like beings that have passed beyond. As your body adjusts and expands, you will see more and more of the spiritual world.

The Christ force is coming to earth in greater potency and strength than ever before and the end of the old material world will change. The wars, diseases, hatred and selfishness of the mass mind will go through drastic changes, as the Christ power is very strongly at work now. Many groups have predicted the end of the world and believe wholeheartedly that it is coming. They were not taught the basic truth and science of life and how the creative power works. The true meaning of the Christ and the reality of the teachings were not given completely. In one breath they will tell you that when you are ready for the truth, it will be given to you, and in the next breath they will say that the inner teachings are for the select few. If a person is not able to understand a truth, then why worry about trying to cover up anything or to hide it under a cloak of mystery? Just put it out there and make it accessible and those who are ready will be able to understand and accept it.

Jesus taught everything openly, even though many teachings were in parables or allegories. The teachings the world was not ready for were taught in parables. These were given to prepare you for the coming of the Christ in your flesh body. For the spirit of Christ must burn out the dross of selfishness in order for you to become as simple as little children. When you rise above your material self in your ascent to God, you are made so simple that the love of God embraces you. When the love of God enters you, it is occupied only with itself and the power of God, above the practice of any virtue. It is then that you are transformed and die in Christ to yourself and to all separate individuality. It is in this embrace - an essential unity with God through Christ – that all devoted spirits become one with God by a living immersion and melting away into God. And thus is the marriage performed.

God's spirit unites with us through grace in one essence. Our minds, our lives and our essences are simply lifted up and united to the very truth of God. This is the marriage brought about through contemplation with the one life and one spirit of God. This is the contemplative life. In this highest stage of development, the soul is united to the Creator and the Self is found. All of a sudden, without difficulty, without stress, we see our Self and we just are. It is at this point that we begin to be part of the Edenic state of mind and are in contact with superconsciousness.

True servants of God worship with constant zeal, deep faith and trust. They are non-demanding, pure, just, impartial, devoid of fear, and have forsaken interest in the results of their actions. They do not find fault, do not covet, they are equal-minded with friend or enemy. They are the same in honor and dishonor, in cold and heat, in pain and pleasure, and not attached to outcomes, unaffected by blame or praise. They speak only what is necessary, content with whatever happens, they have no fixed habitation and their heart is firmly fixed on God and full of devotion. Those who seek this sacred ambrosia, the religion of immortality, are the most loved of God.

There is one way. When you approach the door, it will be almost a total darkness, for there will seem to be no door, but a darkened arch, as you approach it. You cannot see beyond it, nor can you make up what your imagination might see. Your spiritual sight cannot penetrate that door. Only when you step through it with absolute faith that this is what you are going to do, will you experience the light of Christ. And it is only through the work and love of the teacher that you can have that door opened, so it is possible for you to see beyond. This is the great way and there is no other.

It is difficult to describe your experience when you have passed through, because everyone is at a different stage of development. You may have had the door of Realization opened in this life so you could experience it, but you might have had this experience for the first time many lifetimes ago.

Sometimes it only requires that you be conscious of that door for it to be opened and the teacher to remove the veil. The past memory is wiped out of your mind to make it easier for you to come in this time. Seek, and you shall find; knock, and it shall be opened.

There is a difference between a problem you have made for yourself and one that is necessary for your spiritual development. You often make things more difficult by fighting everything that comes to you. About 75% of your troubles are not problems at all. None of you are angels, which is good, because you wouldn't be able to stand living here if you were. We are looking for people who have the intelligence, the integrity and the faith to put themselves next to the opening of the door and step through it on absolute faith. That is the only way you will put your foot on the great way. When you do, then you will know and understand.

When you learn to pass out of your physical body, you will find there is total darkness at the crown, and you step through. You move through it even though it is impossible to see through it. This is why most people do not go out of their bodies consciously because they can't stand that feeling of having to let go of everything that is solid earth. On the Way, there are many places you will go that are not solid. It is just as solid there as it is here, except when you look at it from here, it doesn't look solid there. But when you look at here from there, then you have a little bit of a longing. You have to get this idea that you must let go. Anyone who reaches a true spiritual experience will feel extremely light and unstable. You will feel off the earth plane, because you are not used to using your mind as a control. Your control over your spiritual body is entirely dependent upon your knowing. When you try to let go and move out of your body, or if you go out of your physical vehicle - which very often is the way it happens - don't get frightened and fluffy because you haven't got concrete pavement under your feet. A teacher might come to you from the other side trying to get you to let go. You won't need it if you have a concrete idea you are holding on to, which is much stronger.

Letting go of the dense world is the hardest thing for people to do. Once you have entered the way, you will no longer cling to what you have created here. You will use the light and it will become your tool and it will be useful for you. Shining light will become part of what you do in service to the Master and the Mother, for the Creator. Entering the way brings you to an experience where absolute faith without practically any knowing is essential. In the Christian religions the ministers leave loopholes that make allowances for not really connecting to God or being on the way. They allow for mistakes but do not make strong disciples. Only when you carve it out of the rock of reality and build it on the Self, the great being within, can you stand up straight no matter what gale force winds blow around you. If you have decided to depend on the physical things around you, then you haven't reached it yet. You haven't placed your feet firmly on the way, even though the door to Realization has been opened, because you haven't realized the unseen world yet. You don't yet know the difference between here and there and you have not put your faith in what you have been taught or what the Self tells you.

Now don't expect the Self to give you accurate answers when you get in the way all the time. Because if you are talking to me outside of a window, and right when you were about to answer a question I asked, I shut the window, I probably wouldn't hear your answer very accurately. The answers start to come and you get an idea of something that you don't like, and then you close the window and get some rumblings and make something else out of it. Or nothing happens. Well, you are just about as far off track as you can be, because you are still trying to give yourself the answers. The Self is inside wondering, "What's wrong with this creature that I am carrying? Where did she get all the authority?" Well, she didn't get it, she took it. That is a big problem with most people. You usurp the authority, whether it's right or wrong, and use it. Resentment shows up many times when it doesn't quite work the way you would have wanted it to, because you are in the way.

There is a point when you get to the door and begin to see a little sunshine and feel a little warmth. You begin to realize that this is something you have not experienced before, because it is different than anything you have gone through. You may be tempted to put your foot halfway through the door, but you can't do that. There is no easing yourself into Self-Realization, you have to go all the way through at one time. You can't ease into it. It is like someone who goes to a diving school and learns all the gymnastics and training of muscles. Then they come to having to dive and do some really beautiful work on the diving board by the pool. They get up and bounce a couple of times and then stay right there. They can't let go of the diving board and let themselves go into the water.

You're not going to get into the spiritual life either until you let go of the earth. You cannot travel the way while you are fastened to the earth. All the talk we have done about letting go has been a preamble to the "Great Let Go" when you completely let it all go. It doesn't make any difference who your teacher is; you are not going to go through until you do this.

The process is analogous to going down a hallway with many doors. Each is bright and alluring, each lighter and lighter until you reach the darkened door. Some of you will back away from this door and not enter, others will start opening various other doors and going in and looking around. The doors open quite easily and contain some interesting and amusing things. They are the side rooms along the way and

270

you can really get lost in these tangential chambers. When you approach the darkened door, there is just plain nothing there, and it means you have to go through and let go of everything in order to pass through.

If you talk to people who have dabbled on the spiritual path and heard various lecturers and instructors, they will tell you fascinating things that you can get all wrapped up in. They will tell you what they have read and heard. But practically no one talks about what they have attained, what has been healed, who has been transformed or who has been regenerated. This is because they looked into the side rooms on the way down the hall and one can stay amused there for a long, long time. The same holds true when you first start training. The first exercise you are given is to help you control your mind and what you are thinking about. We told you how important it is to control your mind. These little rooms off the hallway are just like recesses of your mind that keep you busy and bring a whole boatload of troubles.

In the New Testament it says that the mind becomes weary of much reading. We go down the central pathway and we dive off the diving board into the pool. You make the third bounce and then you let go and dive in. Then life begins and the regeneration starts. Then you experience the Way becoming narrow. You dedicate your life to the service of human beings and desire to give people what Jesus and Mary and the Creator have given to you. In comparison to the whole solar system, the way is extremely narrow, especially when you compare it to all the antechambers of interesting things to think about. When you get on the Way, you will discover your vision becoming extremely clear and you can see far off. You are no longer blinded by time or space. You can see everyone without any disturbance, feeling or prejudice. You have not given up yourself totally until you can. When you give yourself over to this, you find that the Sun shines all the time. This can be very hard for those who have been indoctrinated by churchianity because they are so used to being in gloom and shadows. They are so used to limiting themselves, that it has become a habit. Even though they can let go, they have to learn to stand in the sunshine all the time.

A man was going up the path and had been walking for a long time when he sat down underneath a tree alongside the path viewing the scenery. He was enjoying himself very much and wasn't in too much of a hurry. You don't get in a hurry when you're out of the way because you have all the time in the world. There's no real hurry, because you will accomplish just as much sitting as moving. He spotted this other man coming along laboring with his load. He was struggling with a great big pack on his back, all doubled up. He called him and said, "Friend, come sit down in the shade with me. You sure have a tremendous load you're carrying, haven't you?" The man said, "Yeah, it's pretty rough." So he said, "Are you sure that is the same pack you started with?" "Sure, it looks like the same pack I started with. I am going to carry it up to the top of the hill." The man said, "Well, would you mind if I looked in it?" The other said, "No, I don't care. I know what's in it, but you can look for yourself if you want to." So he unbuckled it and took it off the carrier on his back, looked in and said, "What's all your laboring for?" The other said, "Why, I've been carrying that pack a long way up the hill. I know how heavy it is." He said, "Well, look." He turned it upside down and shook it. The other man said, "Wait, Wait, Wait. Where did you put it? All those things that I had to carry up the hill with me, where are they?" The man said, "Look, there's nothing there in your pack at all." The other man said, "You mean I've been carrying that dumb thing all the way up the hill and it was only my imagination?" "That's right. If you want to carry the load, you can. I'll give your pack back to you."

That is what most people do. You get in such a habit of carrying the load, you even keep it after you go through Realization and put your feet on the way. You have such a hard time trying to get rid of your pack, because it's been on your back all your life. You have difficulty letting go of the past, which is also part of your pack that you carry. When you really start training spiritually, we keep you so busy that you do not have a chance to get into much mischief. Start looking at the pack you are carrying and make sure there is really something in it. In reality, if you look, you will find that there is very little inside of it. It's just hard for you to get used to not carrying it. Jesus said, **"My yoke is light."** He didn't explain what he meant, but it was very plain. If you will carry the light along with you, you won't have much of a pack to carry.

You have gotten so used to crucifying yourselves that you can't let go of it. If you are going to walk alongside those who have dropped their burdens, you will not be able to keep up if you are carrying stuff in your pack. They dropped them long ago because there is no place for carrying burdens on the spiritual path. You may go through some initiations or gain greater Realization that might put you through some things, but there is no place for carrying a burden. Jesus did that for us and we do not need to do it again. You have to get used to traveling light, and that is difficult for you sometimes. If you desire to travel along swiftly, you must drop your burdens. There is too much to do after you get on the Way to sit down and muddle over crazy ideas that you used to have. The most important experience in the world is the illumination and the Self-Realization on the great way. Jesus said to the rich man, **"Go sell everything and follow me."** Not tomorrow, not the day after, but today. Now! And I'll show you the dominion of Heaven.